MW01110404

Jesus
the
Outlaw

WANTED
Dead or Alive

Jesus
the
Outlaw

WANTED
Dead or Alive
Tom Bruno

Bridge-Logos *Publishers*

Gainesville, Florida 32614 USA

JESUS THE OUTLAW
by Tom Bruno

ISBN # 0-88270-872-4
Library of Congress Catalog Card: Pending

Published by:
Bridge-Logos *Publishers*
Gainesville, FL 32614

DEDICATION

This book is dedicated to two professors at Western Theological Seminary that taught me more than books ever could: to the late John Piet who spent ten years of his ministry in India. He was the first to teach me what it means to be an outlaw for Jesus.

And to Dr. Richard Oudersluys, who enlightened me with his patience, knowledge, and wisdom during my first years of seminary.

AUTHOR'S NOTE

No statements in this book are written
with the intention of being anti-Semitic.
The words "Jews," "religious leaders,"
"Pharisee," and "Sanhedrin" are meant
to be understood in the historical
context in which they were written."
—Thomas A. Bruno

Contents

Introduction xi

1. The Death of the Outlaw 1
2. The Birth of the Outlaw 9
3. Outlaw Without a Home 19
4. John the Baptist, Outlaw 29
5. The Issues That Made Jesus
   an Outlaw 39
6. The Plot to Discredit Jesus,
   the Outlaw 53
7. The Plot to Murder Jesus,
   the Outlaw 61
8. Jesus Warns His Disciples About
   Becoming Outlaws 67
9. The Outlaw Invades the Temple 77
10. Judas Betrays the Outlaw 85
11. The Outlaw and the Courageous
    Coward 93
12. Two Outlaws Named Jesus 99
13. The Outlaw in the Borrowed
    Tomb 105
14. The Outlaw Lives Again! 109
15. From Outlaw Hunter to Outlaw 115
16. The Disciples Become Outlaws 125
17. Jesus, Still an Outlaw 139
18. The Death of the Outlaw, Revisited 147

ACKNOWLEDGEMENTS

Several individuals have been helpful in the publishing of this book. The entire crew at Bridge encouraged me from the beginning to develop this concept of *Jesus, the Outlaw*. My special thanks goes to Marianne Graves, who is part of the Bridge staff, who listened to parts of this manuscript in its early stages, and to Cindy Crosby, my editor, who has once again taken my pile of information and made something special of it.

My children and their mates: Chris and Ed, Tom and Sue, and Matthew and Debra have all been supportive of my writing endeavors.

Dr. Mike Fonfara has been a constant source of information and encouragement that this was an idea whose time had come.

My special friend, Bobbie Henderson read the first entire manuscript and gave me some excellent guidance. She always patiently listened to me ramble on about a new discovery.

My love and gratitude to Michele, my wife, who unselfishly allows me the time to be alone and write at all times of the day and night.

OUTLAW

Someone who is not protected by the law
Someone who is outside of the law
Someone who has committed crimes against the
state or the people.

INTRODUCTION

About three weeks after Easter, I wandered into a religious bookstore. On the sale table was a sign in bold letters that read, "Crosses and crucifixes half-price." We could hang the same sign on twenty-first century Christianity. We make faith easy. We make it cheap. Think about it—for many, the Christian faith costs only ten-percent of their after-tax income and a few hours of religious ceremony.

Suffer? We know no suffering—our faith is one of convenience and comfort. Everything from the construction of the pews to the time of worship is centered on the worshipper.

Religion is acceptable, even admirable as long as it's a "Sunday" thing. Soul, spirituality, and connectedness are the buzzwords of our society, but their connotation is vague. The 'god' they describe is formless—without definition. Today's spiritualists lead us to an Eastern-mystical experience that precludes the God of Abraham, Isaac, and Jacob. Meditation, self-awareness, and righteous living, in and of themselves leave the soul empty and certainly do not point us to Jesus. Modern solutions focus on a cheap imitation of true Christian faith!

Not only that but Christians who know truth of Christ, more often than not fail in sharing that truth because of timidity. For example, a young man and his fiancée came to see me for premarital counseling. Since I knew she was a Christian, I asked how God would be a part of their marriage. Without hesitation the man told me that he was an atheist. I was not ready for his answer. I was caught off-guard, and as a result gave a poor defense for Christianity. But he was prepared. . . he was sure of himself and proud of his counter-current stance. After the couple left, I realized how backward the confrontation was—Christians must be as bold or bolder than those who claim there is no God.

Why is there no richness, no substance to our faith? In an effort to accept in "Christian love" we've become complacent. We no longer confront our society with truth, because we have become lax in learning truth. We no longer shape and mold society, rather, society shapes and molds us. In Jesus, Ph.D. Psychologist, I said, "If you have never been frightened by the teachings of Jesus, perhaps you have not understood them." Not only do we fail to confront society, but we fail to confront the uncomfortable parts of what we claim to believe. Instead we've accepted a popular, feel-good, anything goes religion. Many 'followers' of the Christian faith remain completely unaware of how the outlawish treatment of Christ should affect them.

Jesus was never complacent. Instead, He bucked status quo and was branded a renegade. His teachings, indeed his very presence, inflamed the hatred of kings and religious authorities. If you want a faith with sticking-power, if you search for truth, if you are tired of wishy-washy theology, come, look anew at Jesus—Jesus the outlaw.

CHAPTER ONE

THE DEATH OF THE OUTLAW

LONG AFTER I AWOKE HIS FACE HAUNTED ME . . .

I watched as He fell down upon one knee, overcome by the weight of the rough wooden beams that dug into His back and shoulders. The crowd stirred as they watched His pain. A Roman soldier ordered, "Stay back!" as he shoved me into the crowd.

I lost my balance and fell into a priest who stood arms smugly crossed. I excused myself and then asked, "Who is the man carrying the cross? What is his crime?"

1

"He's a charlatan, He claims to be the Son of God," he scoffed.

At my left, a man spat into the dirt, then cursed, "Nothing good comes out of Nazareth!"

I looked back at the pitiful figure, immobilized, seemingly frozen in time. He certainly didn't appear threatening now.

"He is the Messiah! I cannot forget his healing. Only the Messiah could heal me. He truly is the Messiah," wept a man behind me. Over and over he repeated himself. No one could quiet him.

"What is His name?" I asked.

"Jesus the Nazarene," another voice mocked.

A soldier pushed forward and caught the cross before it crushed the man called Jesus. He scanned the crowd and then pointed a callused finger at a Jewish bystander.

"You there, what is your name?" he sneered.

"Who, me?" The Jewish man appeared startled and a bit fearful at being singled out of the crowd.

"Yes, you, what is your name?" Barked the soldier.

The man hesitated, then answered "Simon."

"Get over here, pick up this cross!"

Simon stepped forward and with the help of the soldiers, maneuvered the awkward load of the cross onto his back. The crowd rallied at the increasing drama of the situation. They encouraged this healthy, muscular man who now carried the cross with comparative ease, as if he had done some great feat. Yet there were no words of encouragement for the original bearer of the cross.

The Roman soldier gave the order and the procession began to move again.

The crowd pushed and shoved to watch the spectacle in the street. Some insulted Jesus. A few cried. Several stood bewildered and silent.

So this was Jesus. I had heard about Him. Who hadn't? People said he was a miracle-man or a prophet. I even heard he had raised a man from the dead. Some thought he was the Messiah.

I kept pushing, straining to see his face, but his eyes remained fixed on the dirt road. The group stopped again as a Roman soldier tied a rope around Jesus' neck as if He were a dog. The soldier yanked on the makeshift leash and they headed off again.

I elbowed my way to the front of the crowd, as they were about to pass me. Jesus lifted his head. I gasped when I looked at him. A circle of thorns dug into his skull. Fresh blood trickled from his forehead down his face, adding layers to the scabs forming over his beardless jaw. His blood and sweat plastered his long brown hair to the sides of his face. It hung in knotted strands. His entire sun-browned body was covered with sweat from the physical exertion required to continue moving forward.

I though he might fall again as he paused, but instead He looked at me. His eyes—dark, penetrating, and intense—met mine. His lips parted, as if he was going to tell me something. As I waited, unable to breathe, for what He had to say, I felt I had known him all my life. Without a word passing between us, we had connected. I needed to touch him, to embrace him. My doubts about his claims disappeared as I was drawn to him with strange intensity.

As I reached toward him a whip from one of the soldiers lashed across his back. "Keep moving," the soldier commanded. Jesus' eyes left mine as he continued stumbling down the narrow street leading to a hill called Golgotha, just outside the city. The hill of death, used by the Roman authorities for many of their executions, a cursed land.

Unable shake the penetrating look of Jesus' eyes I followed him up the hill. At the top two other criminals were being tied to the beams of the crucifixion crosses. They cursed and spat and struggled against the soldiers.

Jesus of Nazareth stood motionless in the middle of all the commotion. The Romans ripped off his soiled, tattered garment, reopening his wounds and leaving Him stripped before the crowd. The deep cuts, which criss-crossed his back, flowed once more with sticky blood.

Two soldiers came forward, one with a hammer, and the other with several one-foot spikes. I closed my eyes momentarily, wanting to shut out the scene, but unable to escape the sound of the hammer and the nails. Metal upon metal. Flesh and bones and the splitting of wood. With every few blows came a muted thud, where the hammer missed the nail and bruised the arm instead.

And yet through all of this no curse left Jesus' lips.

The women wept. My own cheeks were wet with tears. We were participants, all of us. Participants in death.

"Oh my God, why?" I asked.

The cross was raised high, positioned over a pre-dug hole, and dropped into place. Jesus' body lunged forward and the flesh at his hands and feet tore from the weight of his body. He winced in silent agony.

The crowd as if awakened from their trance began to shout curses again. Several priests shook their fists at Him angrily, shouting, "Do you think you are the Son of God now?" Others jeered, "Come down from the cross and save Yourself!"

Others like myself stood mesmerized, helpless, and dejected.

When I could look no longer, I turned to notice a group of women weeping. One woman cried inconsolably, "My son, my son, my beloved son!" I looked at Jesus, who faintly smiled at her through His pain; she must be His mother.

Jesus uttered some words softly, but I couldn't make out what they were. A wind stirred the stillness. Black clouds rolled in, and the once bright day darkened within minutes—even the earth disapproved. Thunder rumbled, and a bolt of lightning streaked across the sky. The ground shook. The crowd looked uneasy, then alarmed. With another crack of thunder and the beginning of a pelting rain, the people scattered to shelter. Yet who could remain sheltered from the image of this man who hung dying.

The Roman guard next to me shook his head and whispered in awe "Surely this is the Son of God."

There was no shelter for me, so I stood, the rain beating against my face. I knew my life would never be the same. I had so many questions to ask, so many 'whys' I needed answered. I looked at Him once more, and as if He knew my questions He lifted His eyes and saw into my soul.

My body trembled as it came out of sleep. His pleading eyes haunted me. Jesus, crucified as a criminal, the death of an outlaw.

CHAPTER TWO

"Every year at Christmas time Christians prepare
for the birth of Jesus with a trip to the mall."

THE BIRTH OF THE OUTLAW

Where do outlaws come from? Most would argue trace their background or blame society as the source of their lawlessness. But in the case of the Christ, he was anything, but lawless. And even as a child he was hunted.

But Jesus' birth was more than a bit inconvenient. It was riddled with problems from the beginning. Mary and Joseph were the average happy couple. Joseph asked Mary's father for her hand in marriage. When the dowry or mohar had been given, Mary's father gave his permission and the period of betrothal began. The betrothal time period, which could be as long as a year, was to be a time of getting acquainted without sexual intimacy. Such intimacy or consummation only occurred after the wedding ceremony. Then Mary told Joseph she was pregnant. Mary had pled, "God did it!" But Joseph could not believe.

Joseph knew they had not been sexually intimate, and even though Mary swore that she had remained chaste—there was no earthly way for the baby to come from thin air. Joseph being a kind and righteous man, planned to end their betrothal quietly (Matthew 1:19). According to the Law, the lack of physical intimacy did not lessen the obligation or recognized rights of the betrothed couple. So people considered Mary to be Joseph's wife, and Joseph her husband. Thus the only way to dissolve their union would be divorce.

As Mary's near-husband, Joseph had the right to use the full extent of the law against her obvious infidelity. Adultery was punishable by death. Or Joseph could have taken Mary to the

priest for the rite of bitter water, described in
Numbers 5:11-31. The priest would give the
accused a drink of water, and if she was guilty of
infidelity, the water would turn bitter in her
stomach causing much suffering. "Her abdomen
will swell and her thigh waste away and she will
become accursed among her people." (Numbers
5:27). The Protevangel of the James, one of the
earliest apocryphal books of the Christian
Church, claim that Mary did go through this test.

But God protects His Son by sending an
angel to confirm with Joseph that "what is
conceived in her is from the Holy Spirit."
(Matthew 1:20b). From that moment, Joseph
fully accepts Mary as having been faithful to him.
This acceptance on the part of Joseph towards
Mary is pivotal to God's planned Christmas story.

If Joseph had set Mary apart from him with
a divorce, Jesus would have become an illegitimate
child, which would have made him an outcast,
illegitimate, and an outlaw for the wrong reason.
Kingdoms have been refused to heirs, their only
'sin' being one they couldn't control. But Jesus
becomes the legitimate son of Mary, a virgin, and
son of Joseph his 'adoptive' father.

From the moment Jesus Christ entered this world He caused a stir. Angels sang at his birthplace, shepherds came and worshipped. And far away wise men discovered a new star, which they began to follow as they searched for a King.

The Roman senate appointed King Herod as King of Judea in 40 BC. This heathen Gentile ruthlessly ruled his territory with an iron hand. The people of Jerusalem snickered it was safer to be Herod's pig than his son! He married four times, and due to irreconcilable differences, killed one wife, three sons, one mother-in-law, and one brother-in-law. On his deathbed, he ordered that all the Jewish leaders be rounded up and herded into a stadium. As he died he commanded that the Jewish leaders be killed. Fortunately, the order was not carried out.

It was this Herod that reigned during the birth of Christ. As per normal for the Roman government, Herod kept watch for possible rebellions against the established order. Religious zealots were ignored, but political opponents were squashed. The recent rebellions of Spactucus and the Maccabees were still fresh in the Roman authority's minds.

So when the Magi came to Herod in search of new King, Herod summoned them into his presence. The Magi witnessed an unusual consolation of stars in the sky, and followed it to Judea, and then to Jerusalem, where they inquired of the religious leaders where such a birth would occur.

Who were these Magi? The term "Magi" comes from Persia. The Magi belonged to a chaste group of priests who believed in astrology. The earliest mention of the word "Magi" is found in Daniel 2:2,10, and is used in a negative manner suggesting affiliations with magic and sorcery. But in the book of Matthew, the term "Magi" doesn't have these negative implications.

Tertullian, was an early church writer who called the Magi "Kings," assumed that since there were three gifts there must have been three wise men. Later, around 600 AD the Armenian Infancy Gospel gives the wise men names: Melkon, Bathasar, and Gaspar.

The Magi's conclusions about the star were correct, regardless of the specifics about their origin. They were determined to find the King, but little did they know they were setting disastrous events in motion.

The scriptures tell of the common people, the angels, and the Gentiles who came to worship, but what is not recorded is an account of a Jewish leader who searched the Christ. Despite the information from the wise men, despite the answers they gave, the leaders only informed the King of the inquiries. It was business as usual. Their attitude of indifference was a foreshadowing of the religious leaders' attitudes throughout Jesus ministry. Their indifference grew into anger and anger into the motivation to commit murder. Jesus commented on their rejection during His final days quoting scripture saying: "Oh Jerusalem, Jerusalem, you who kill the prophets and stone those sent to you, how often I have longed to gather your children together, as a hen gathers her chicks under wings, but you were not willing" (Matthew 23:37).

Herod gave the Magi instructions, making them believe his intentions were pure. "Go and make a careful search for the child. As soon as you find him, report to me, so that I too may go and worship him" (Matthew 2:8). Herod wanted them to do the work and come back with the location of this new King.

As we carefully read the scriptures we discover some interesting facts not usually included in the Christmas story. First, the Magi clearly appear after Jesus is born. This is evident in Matthew 2:1 which says "After Jesus was born in Bethlehem in Judea, during the time of King Herod, Magi from the East came to Jerusalem...." Notice also that Jesus is not referred to as a baby in the manger as used in the Gospel of Luke but the Greek word suggesting "child" is used to describe Him. The Gospel of Matthew describes it this way, "On coming to the house, they saw the child with his mother Mary and they bowed and worshipped him. Then they opened their treasures and presented him with gifts of gold and of incense and of myrrh. And having been warned in a dream not to go back to Herod, they returned to their country by another route" (Matthew 2:11-12). Notice that the word house is used instead of manger, and that nothing is mentioned of Joseph at that particular incident.

The term wise men appears to be appropriate. Wisely they sought the new King, wisely they followed the star, and wisely they listened to the warning of an angel who warned them not to go back to Herod. They returned back to their homeland using a different route, undetected by Herod's spies.

Immediately after the wise men leave, Joseph is warned in a dream by an angel that he must take Mary and Jesus into Egypt. This is the only place they will be safe from the tyranny of Herod. They remain there until the death of Herod in 4 BC.

Herod did not count on God intervening in his plans. When He discovered that he had been outwitted it was too late. Herod was furious! He was used to being in control, and was rarely outwitted — especially by foreigners. Herod knew that if this new King were allowed to mature into a man, he would risk his throne. So Herod acted— swift and brutal. He ordered all male children under two years old to be killed in Bethlehem and the surrounding vicinity.

The judgment of Herod is swift and brutal. He orders all male children under two to be killed in Bethlehem and the surrounding vicinity. The Roman Catholic Church still celebrates the holy day, Slaughter of the Innocents, in remembrance of this event. We don't know how many innocent children were murdered to kill this one threat, but we do know the evil order was carried out. Jesus outlawed even at as toddler.

After the danger is past, an angel tells Joseph that the threat is over and he and his family can return to Judea. In a fourth appearance, an angel through a dream Joseph back to their final dwelling place in the district of Galilee. ". . . [Joseph] went and lived in a town called Nazareth. So was fulfilled what was said through the prophets: "He will be called a Nazarene" (Matthew 2:23). Without such angelic interventions by God, Jesus would not have survived his first few years.

Who is this person, not a man, but a child—feared by enemies so greatly that many are killed to weed him out? Before he speaks full sentences, He is feared. Before he performs one miracle, He is outlawed. Before he preaches one sermon, He is hunted.

Applications from the Outlaw

Today, we celebrate Christmas by joyously singing "Silent Night," reading the sacred words of the Christmas story, lighting the Advent candles, and gathering for worship. It is a pleasant time to remember a wee-babe in a manger with fluffy animals all around. But we must not forget the blood of the first Christmas. We must not forget the deceit of Herod and the courage, persistence, and wisdom of the wise men. The enemies of Jesus did not want him to grow up. Unfortunately, many that claim to follow Him won't allow Him to grow up either. By keeping Him as a baby in a manger, He remains ineffective. Many of us have not gotten beyond the Jesus of the Christmas story.

Don't let the story of Christmas become business as usual.

Loving Father, Help me to always make room for your Son into my life. Never let me get so busy, so complacent that I forget that my life with You and Your Son is not an acceptance of beliefs and ideas, but the entering into a living relationship.

CHAPTER THREE

"Not even His brothers believed that Jesus was the
Messiah He claimed to be.
In truth, they were embarrassed by Him!"

OUTLAW WITHOUT A HOME

During my teenage years, my mother and
father separated. The separation tore me from the
security of my home in Poughkeepsie, New York,
and placed me into a foster home for one year.
After that year, my mother, my brother, Jim, and
I moved to Grand Rapids, Michigan, where we
settled down for several years. With all the
changes in location I never had the chance to say
goodbye to my friends in New York.

One summer, I went back home to stay with my best friend, Dan. I was excited about the trip and filled with great expectation! I soon realized, however, that there was something missing. My friends had moved on with their lives, our relationships had changed. Emptiness haunted me for a long time after that visit, I had lost a part of my identity. At fourteen years old, I discovered that when you leave, you can never return home.

When Jesus let the people back home know he was coming back for a visit, Mary, the mother of Jesus, must have been excited! I can picture Mary's face beaming with pride, knowing that her beloved son, God's anointed Messiah, was coming home.

Nazareth was a substantial city even in the time of Jesus. We often think of Jesus as a backwoods boy, raised outside the mainstream Jewish life. Not true! Nazareth was termed a "polis," which means that it could have had a population as large as 20,000 people. The word "Nazareth" translates as "watchtower." It was situated at about 1,600 feet, high above the valleys around it. From the city, one could look out to Mount Carmel where Elijah had fought against the prophets of Baal. Nearby is the spot where Jehu slaughtered Jezebel. A short distance away, there was the road that led from Egypt to Damascus, the road that led to Jerusalem, as well as the caravan road from Arabia to the outer frontier parts of the Empire, used by traders. The land was rich and fertile, and wild flowers and fruit flourished. Nazareth was also situated in part of the southerly limestone hills of the Labanon range.

This was the city Jesus came home to, the place he had lived at least twenty-eight years. Can you imagine how he felt and what he thought as he approached Nazareth? He knew these people, he had grown up here. However, Jesus was about to find out that you can't go back home again. Those left behind usually remember your faults and weaknesses—in fact, they never forget them!

Instead of heading for his family's house, Jesus went to the synagogue to worship. He planned this trip to Nazareth as a springboard for His ministry. It was appropriate for Jesus to speak at the synagogue. It represented His ministry and those who listened hopefully would spread His message, and the synagogue was an excellent place to find a multitude of people.

At the service, the Scriptures of the Old Testament were read in Hebrew. These Scriptures were not found in books, written on scrolls, and stored in a special place within the sanctuary. Only the Rabbi or a special attendant known as a Chazzan would have access to the sacred text. After reading the verses in Hebrew, a male Jew would give the exact translation in Aramaic or a language the common worshipers in Nazareth would understand.

The reading of Isaiah for that day could have been specifically assigned or chosen directly by Jesus. In any case it is the scroll of Isaiah that is handed to Him, and it is the powerful verses in Isaiah 61:1-2 that He reads, describing the Messiah.

> *"The Spirit of the Lord is on me,*
> *because he has anointed me*
> *to preach good news to the poor*
> *He has sent me to proclaim freedom for the prisoners*
> *and recovery of sight for the blind,*
> *to release the oppressed,*
> *to proclaim the year of the Lord's favor."*
> Isaiah 61:1,2 (see also Luke 4:18-19)

When Jesus finished the reading of the Scriptures, He rolled it up and gave it back to the attendant or the Rabbi, and then sat down. It was appropriate to read a Biblical text while standing, to show reverence for the Holy writings, but anyone who was going to teach would do so while sitting. As Jesus began to teach the Bible says "the eyes of everyone in the synagogue were fastened on him." I am sure they wondered what he would say about these verses on the Messiah. Imagine the excitement of the moment!

All of Israel waited for the coming King, so scripture on the Messiah was often discussed. It seemed that all the rulers had their own opinion. Many a proud mother hoped that perhaps her son would be the chosen one. The Bible says that Jesus had just come from Capernaum and records that Jesus had already performed many miracles. His fame and reputation preceded Him to his hometown. So the townspeople in the synagogue that day felt they had a celebrity in their presence.

Jesus knew they desired to see Him perform mighty works in Nazareth, but He refused to do so. Scripture says that the people in Nazerath begged him to "'Do here in your hometown what we have heard that you did in Capernaum'" (Luke 4:23). They asked for a sign . . . so that they could boast about Jesus.

Jesus recognized their lack of faith. And refused to respond positively affirming their disbelief. That is when He shared an eternal gem, "I tell you this truth," he said. "No prophet is accepted in his hometown" (Luke 4:24). Jesus went on to declare, "Today this scripture is fulfilled in your hearing" (Luke 4:21). Everyone's eyes in the synagogue must have been fixed on Him! He was telling them, "Yes, I am the Messiah." Jesus had just exploded the biggest bombshell that the devout worshipers of the synagogue could hear.

There were two immediate reactions from those who heard Him. First, they were amazed that He declared Himself to be the Messiah. "Isn't this Joseph's son?" they asked. With their comments they brought Him to their earthly level and refused to see Him as anything more than the boy down the street. They could not imagine anything special about Jesus, because they had seen him grow up. They knew his brothers, his sisters, and his parents, Mary and Joseph.

Then Jesus says something that pushes them right over the edge. It turns their amazement into anger and fury. He says, "I assure you that there were many widows in Israel in Elijah's time, when the sky was shut for three-and-a-half years and there was a severe famine throughout the land. Yet Elijah was not sent to any of them, but to a widow in Zarephath in the region of Sidon. And there were many in Israel with leprosy in the time of Elisha the prophet, yet not one of them was cleansed – only Naaman the Syrian" (Luke 4:24-27).

The reaction of those who heard this was swift. They were furious. His listeners believed they were God's chosen people. They despised the Gentiles, believing God would use them as fuel in hell! However, here is Jesus pulling stories from their own history showing two of their greatest prophets blessing two Gentiles. Why? Because in each story he quoted the reason the Gentiles were used was the Israelite faith. When His people were faithless, God favored the faithful—even if they were Gentiles by birth. God refuses to bless the lack of faith. Jesus taught them that because of their lack of faith He would take His message to the Gentiles. The gift of God, Jesus said, is for those who believe – whoever they may be!

The crowd turned violent. "Who is this young Jesus that has grown up before our eyes, who now claims that the Gentiles will be favored over the Jews?" they said, angrily. They questioned his brothers. The replied that Jesus was not the Messiah, but their brother. The Gospel writer John flatly states, "For even his own brothers did not believe in him." (John 7:5).

At this moment Jesus stands alone. The worshipers of the synagogue got up and drove Him out of the synagogue. They drove Jesus before them until they came to the top of the hill that the town was built upon. They planned to throw Him over the cliff – a drop of at least 2000 feet. They would not stand for his blasphemy; they wanted Jesus dead!

A huge crowd gathered around Jesus, shouting at him, working themselves into frenzy. A mob mentality developed as they began shouting, "Kill him!" Nothing He said could be heard above the cry of the mob.

Jesus turned and looked at them. The crowd grew silent and stood immobile. They could not move toward Him; they could not lay one finger on Him, because His time had not come. He walked toward them and then was gone.

The Bible does not record another instance of Jesus returning 'home' to Nazareth. Rejected by those who knew Him, misunderstood and mistreated, Jesus left an outlaw to His hometown.

Applications from the Outlaw

Identifying with Jesus may put us at odds with our spouse or someone in our family. We may not find honor and respect at home, where we are reminded of our faults and weaknesses. We may be outlaws in our own families and hometowns. There is nothing that we experience that Jesus did not experience during His earthly existence! Jesus has promised to give us comfort and rest, to be our family. As Christians we are joint-heirs with Christ, He is our brother. May we have the quiet confidence that Jesus showed in the middle of the conflict that can come from close to home.

Prayer

Father, thank for giving me a home with You, so that no matter how I am treated by the world I can always find refuge in You. May I have the courage to know who I am and not shy away when others may not accept me.

Chapter Four

"His message was simple, 'Repent, the Kingdom of God is at hand.'

John knew he was here to get the Spotlight on Jesus. He not only gave it his best shot He lost his head doing it."

John the Baptist, Outlaw

The Castle of Machaerus, one of the residences of Herod Antipas, was a fortress overlooking the east shore of the Dead Sea. Which made it easy to defend, but difficult to attack. Deep within the dungeon of a castle, staples and iron hooks attached to the dank wall held John the Baptist captive. How difficult this captivity is for a man who is a son of the desert, a man use to the fresh air and the open skies, as well as sleeping under the stars of Palestine!

Little is known about John's early years. Scripture simply says, he "grew and became strong in spirit" (Luke 1:80). John dared to speak in public what others would only whisper in private. He told the people to share food and clothing, which was a jab at the materialism of contemporary Israelites. He warned the tax collectors about taking more money than they were entitled. He declared that soldiers should be content with their wages. He criticized the religious and righteous as being too smug. He struck at the greediness of contemporary society. In the wilderness and desert he called the comfortable to come out to repent and be baptized. He cared little for popularity, and instead focused on truth. His clash with Herod Antipas was inevitable.

John's relationship with Jesus was unique. In the Gospel of Luke, we read that the angel Gabriel announced both the birth of Jesus and John. Their mothers were close kinswomen. John and Jesus may have even been playmates! Jesus went to John to be baptized. Although John does not want to baptize Jesus, Jesus insisted that this was appropriate. To his own disciples John declared about Jesus, "Look, the Lamb of God, who takes away the sin of the world!" (John 1:29). According to the Gospel of Mark, Jesus did not begin his ministry until John was arrested. Jesus apparently accepted this as a signal to begin His work.

For a time it may have seemed that the disciples of Jesus and John were in competition. But John makes it clear that his task is to prepare the way for the coming Messiah; he was not the Messiah. John declared to his followers, "I baptize you with water for repentance. But after me will come one who is more powerful than I, whose sandals I am not fit to carry. He will baptize you with the Holy Spirit and with fire." (Matthew 3:11).

As Jesus was baptized, the heavens opened, "He saw the Spirit of God descending like a dove and lighting on Him. And a voice from heaven said, "This is my Son, whom I love; with Him I am well pleased." (Matthew 3:16-17). John pictured himself as the best man at a wedding of which Jesus was the bridegroom (John 3:29).

As events unfolded, John decreased in importance and Jesus increased.

It was in prison that the faith of John was shaken. Perhaps, it was the result of the lonely hours of isolation, which gave John too much time to think. Perhaps he saw his life crumbling, and could not understand the meaning of it. Whatever the reason, John doubted his belief in Jesus. He wondered out loud as to whether Jesus was truly the Christ, the one they had been waiting for. Remember this doubt comes after John had called him the Lamb of God and witnessed the testimony of the Holy Spirit and the approval of God at Jesus' baptism.

God's saints throughout the Bible struggled with doubt as well. One day the great prophet Elijah confronted all of the priests of Baal, and the next day he was depressed and running for his life. One day Peter declared at Caesarea Phillippi that Jesus was the Son of God, and soon after he denied that he ever knew Jesus. Even Jesus, who courageously went to Jerusalem, later fell on His knees asking God to take away the cross.

One day everything looks so clear, and the next everything seems so doubtful. One day faith seems so easy so natural, and the next day we find ourselves in the valley again doubting ourselves and the power of God. Sometimes, the valleys and mountains are so close together! The battlefield is not always outside the body; the battle is within the human heart. As we wrestle with our faith, we sometimes even question "Is He is the One?"

So it was with John, captured in the prison of questions. Despite everything he had said about Jesus, now He wonders if Jesus was the Messiah. So John asks Jesus, "Are you the Messiah? Yes or No?"

The answer of Jesus was characteristically creative. He did not give a simple yes or no answer. Jesus said, "Go back and report to John what you have seen and heard: The blind receive sight, the lame walk, those who have leprosy are cured, the deaf hear, the dead are raised, and the good news is preached to the poor. Blessed is the man who does not fall away on account of me."(Luke 7:23).

Notice that the emphasis of Jesus' response was based on what Jesus was doing. And everything that he did were the deeds of One who was anointed by God. Jesus was doing the work of the Messiah and John clearly understood that message.

Perhaps, there was a personal message here as well for John, "Blessed is the man who does not fall away on account of me." Jesus, I believe, was telling John to be strong, even though he was being treated as an outlaw. Be steadfast, John. Be of good faith! Your faith will be rewarded. Jesus' words were timeless, "The man who does not fall away will be rewarded."

John was at the mercy of three people: Herod Antipas, Herodias, and Salmone. John had dared to openly rebuke Herod for getting rid of his legal wife, then seducing his brother's wife and marrying her. John did not mince words over the immorality of this act. According to the Jewish law in Leviticus 18:16; 20- 21, Herod had entered an adulterous marriage by seducing his brother's wife.

The relationship between John and Herod was a paradox. Herod was a "Dr. Jekyll and Mr.

Hyde" in his treatment of John the Baptist. On one hand, Herod feared and respected John. He was insulted by John's words, and yet Scripture says he enjoyed listening to him. Herod realized that John was a holy and righteous man, so he protected him. He often had John come before him to talk; other times he went into the dungeon, and would sit alone with John and ask him questions. He was fascinated by what John said!

All the while Herodias, was secretly listening, and waiting for an opportunity for vengeance. She hated John the Baptist! He was an embarrassment to her, a thorn in her side that continually reminded her that she was not above the law and was indeed guilty of sin. She would do anything to silence John!

She found her tool for revenge in her young, sensuous daughter. On Herod's birthday, the local government and military commanders were invited to the party, as well as anyone who was important politically. There was a delicious banquet, with lavish entertainment, including a seductive dance from Salome. The now sexually aroused and pleasantly drunk, Herod tells Salome, "Ask me for anything you want, and I'll give it to you—up to half my kingdom."

Salome didn't respond hastily. She inquired of her mother what she should ask for. Herodias didn't have to think about it at all. She had waited for a moment just like this to get back at John.

Salome returned to Herod and asked for the head of John the Baptist.

Caught! Herod was embarrassed. He was forced into doing something he did not want to do. With such an audience of military and powerful guests, he would appear weak not to carry out the request. Yet, was he not weak to respond to someone's wishes simply because of a hasty promise? Was he not weak for refusing to do the right thing in order to 'save face'?

Herod could have told Salome "no," but instead he ordered the execution. As Herodias accepted the head of John from Salome, she received what she wanted; Herod got more than he bargained for.

The disciples of John quickly came, claiming the body of the John the Baptist in order to give him a proper funeral. When Jesus was told about John's death, He withdrew to a place of solitude for reflection on the loss of a loved one and the cost of His mission.

The older I become, the more I am intrigued by the irony of life. What goes around does in fact come around! Like a giant boomerang, if we don't duck it, it can knock us out. Herod asked for something that was forbidden—his brother's wife. He got what he forcibly took. Now, something forbidden would be asked from him— the life of John the Baptist. Legally speaking, it was his to take, but in every other way, it was forbidden. Yet, he gave the order. We read in historical documents that Herod may have been called to Rome to tell why he took the life of John the Baptist without a trial. His own boomerang hit him and it haunted him for eternity.

John's disciples were probably surprised at his death. The disciples of Jesus were surprised at John's death. Jesus was not surprised at all.

Jesus knew the price of being an outlaw.

Applications from the Outlaw

How much are you willing to give up to follow Jesus? John the Baptist gave up everything!

So often, we ask "How little can I get away with?" Then we wonder why we don't get more out of life. We will get in proportion to what we give.

Remember how John began his work, "Repent, for the Kingdom of heaven is near." The message is still relevant for us today, turn from negative, weak and sinful attitudes and behavior and face the living God. Regardless of where you are, how old you are and what you have done, you can turn to God now. God has a better plan and it involves His Son, Jesus.

John the Baptist shows us that being a disciple of Jesus is serious business, not for the weak of heart, but rather for those of faith and courage. Following in Jesus' footsteps isn't easy, but you won't be alone. As you enter into a relationship with Him, ask, "How much can I give?"

A Prayer

God, those who have gone before me have been courageous in their faith. May I also exhibit the faith that will make you pleased to call me Your Child!

CHAPTER FIVE

"Forget it Jesus, we will never believe in you!
When you use the word, 'forgive' We will
always pick up stones to kill you, For you
blasphemy against our laws and traditions.
Only God can forgive. You are a mere man and
nothing more!"
(A paraphrase of some of Jesus' critics)

THE ISSUES THAT MADE
JESUS AN OUTLAW

Ask U. S. Democrats about the presidential
election of 2000 and you are sure to get a heated
commentary about the campaign without having
to speak another word. Ask U.S. Republicans
about the same election and again you are sure to

get a lengthy response, but from a totally different perspective.

Are one-person right, and the other wrong? Is any one of them dishonest? I think not! The reality of the situation depends on the way you see the events of the election and how you interpret them. Thus, Democrats and Republicans will probably never agree on the way the votes were counted during the election of 2000.

The reality we see depends on our orientation. The same principle was at work during the time of Jesus. Some believed. Others remained skeptics.

The issues that separated Jesus and His critics were diverse and complex. Some of the issues seemed insurmountable, while others just differed in approach. Understanding these issues between Jesus and His critics will help us to understand why He so quickly became an outlaw.

There is mystery here. The Pharisees and other religious leaders had the same Old Testament scriptures to read as we do. They were waiting in intense expectation for the Messiah. They had direct contact with Jesus and observed

His life. So what went wrong? Why then did they reject Jesus as the Messiah, when they claimed the Messiah was whom they were waiting for?

Many of the religious leaders were in love with the concept of the Messiah, but they were shocked at the reality of the Messiah. The chase seemed to be better than the catch. I can imagine the long conversations that may have occurred in synagogues and at the temple about the Messiah. They loved the discussion and the stimulating thought.

Despite this, they were not ready for a Messiah that would challenge their religion and their position of power. The actual appearance of the Messiah was bad news. Human nature hasn't changed much! We practice selective listening. We hear what we want to hear; we see what we want to see. We fall in love with the idea of love, rather than the person.

There were two different groups who were opposed to Jesus. The first group was made up of Jews who saw themselves in positions of power they did not want to forfeit. They were part of the High Priest system, or the Sanhedrin, and were at the pinnacle of Jewish politics. The second group was made up of the religious leaders who opposed Jesus for attacking their beliefs. They had political leanings, but they were not politically motivated. They also had genuine religious differences with Jesus. Jesus breaking their religious traditions such as healing on the Sabbath offended them. Jesus' disciples not washing their hands before eating offended them. They were offended by the audacity of His teachings.

In the end, these groups of people put aside their differences to unite behind one thing: They wanted to get rid of Jesus. They wanted him dead!

The political leaders wanted a purely political Messiah, not a spiritual one. They expected a Messiah who would rid them of the Romans. They thought they had everything else under control. The laws and sacrifices were already in place, the temple had been rebuilt, and the prophets had come and gone. The only conceivable problem they thought they had was the Romans. Everything else was in order. Given a Messiah who addressed their real issues, they may have followed.

The religious leaders were proud of their physical and spiritual heritage as descendants of Abraham. They had the scripture that described the Messiah as part of the Trinity, but they either chose not to believe it or rejected the truth when He became reality. *They were not looking for a Messiah who was God — and would not accept one who was.* They wanted a Messiah who was only a physical person with spiritual and religious insights. Anytime Jesus hinted that He was God, their reaction was swift. They picked up stones to stone Him.

Because they were opposed to Jesus, they rejected his miracles. They looked at things selectively. They simply did not see the miracles.

Hard to believe! Think of the opportunity to be with Him on the earth during His ministry. How wonderful it would have been to see the raising of Lazarus from the dead, the healing of the lepers, the feeding of the multitudes. Yet, many who were there did not see anything supernatural or miraculous. They were focused on the letter of the law. They got lost in the literalism, and they missed the power of God.

What most of the Jews agreed on was that the threat to them as a nation and to their spiritual well being was from an outside source, the Romans. They were under a foreign ruler in an occupied country. They yearned for the days of glory of David and Solomon. To Jesus, the threat to the spiritual well being of Israel was from within. The Romans were not the problem at all! Hypocrisy and literalism were the real threats. Their elaborate system of laws had gotten in the way of spirit of God's kingdom.

Surprisingly, Jesus did not come to be religious! He came to be genuine and pure in spirit and truth. He was surrounded by religion. The impurities and transgressions pervading the religious made him sick. He constantly warned His disciples of the leaven of the scribes and Pharisees. Jesus summed up the religious leaders like this: "You travel over land and sea to win a single convert, and when he becomes one, you make him twice as much a son of hell as you are" (Matthew 23:15).

Another area that Jesus and the religious leaders could not agree on was the Sabbath. The word Sabbath in Hebrew actually means "to cease" or "to desist." The Israelites could work six days, but on the seventh, they must rest. The reasoning was that God rested from creation on the seventh day, and that the observance of the Sabbath was a remembrance that they were once slaves in Egypt (Deuteronomy 5:12-15).

The Sabbath was the heart of Jewish religion and the law. As many as thirty-nine various tasks were prohibited in the observance of the Sabbath. Unfortunately, so many small tasks were banned that the observance began to kill the spirit of the law in order to satisfy what was considered the legal requirements. The stage was set for an intense and heated clash between Jesus and the religious leaders.

Jesus often healed on the Sabbath – unthinkable, to a Jew! The Jewish leaders could not see the miracle, because they were so focused on the fact that it occurred on the Sabbath. The common people marveled at the miracle; the scribes and Pharisees debated about the breaking of the Sabbath. Despite their opposition, He continued. In fact, He may have healed on the Sabbath to prove His point!

Luke wrote this account in his Gospel: "One Sabbath, Jesus was going through the grain fields, and his disciples began to pick some heads of grain, rub them in their hands and eat the kernels. Some of the Pharisees asked 'Why are you doing what is unlawful on the Sabbath?' " (Luke 6:1-2). "Then Jesus said to them, 'Son of Man is Lord of the Sabbath'" (Luke 6:5).

On another Sabbath in a synagogue, Jesus encountered a man with a shriveled hand. He knew the Pharisees and teachers of the law were specifically watching Him to see if He would heal on the Sabbath. They were spying on him! Jesus knew what they were thinking. He told the crippled man to stand up in front of the people, which he did. Then Jesus said to them, 'I ask you, which is lawful on the Sabbath: to do good or to do evil, to save life or to destroy it?'" (Luke 6:6-9). Jesus asked the man to stretch out his hand, and He completely restored him. The response from the crowd: "They were furious and began to discuss with one another what they might do to Jesus" (Luke 6:11). In describing the same incident, Mark wrote that in reaction to Jesus healing the man on the Sabbath: "Then the

Pharisees went out and began to plot with the Herodians how they might kill Jesus" (Mark 3:6).

The Herodians were loyal to Herod Antipas, and they believed that cooperation with the Romans, and support of the government , was in their best interest. It was the Herodians who teamed up with the Pharisees to trap Jesus concerning paying taxes to Caesar. Remember the story? Jesus took a coin and asked " 'Whose portrait is this? And whose inscription?' 'Caesar's,' they replied. Then he said to them, 'Give to Caesar, what is Caesar's, and to God what is God's'" (Matthew 22:22). They went away amazed! Their plan was foiled. *The Herodians were fearful that Jesus might upset the political balance of power.* It was natural that they would become allies with the Pharisees who opposed Jesus.

Jesus knew that as the Son of Man, He had authority over the Sabbath. He also believed it was proper to do good on the Sabbath and that the Sabbath was for man to use and enjoy. The Sabbath was meant to serve man not for man to serve the Sabbath.

Here is a list of some of the issues that stood between Jesus and His critics:

- Touching the unclean
- Eating with sinners
- Not washing before eating
- Healing on the Sabbath
- Eating with tax collectors
- Forgiving sins
- Associating with Samaritans.

To the teachers of the law, all of these acts of Jesus were unlawful and would lead to a breakdown of the religious system. To them it would lead to spiritual disaster. Jesus was the disrupter of all the religious men had been taught to hold sacred.

When Jesus used the word 'forgive' it led Him to His most intense clash with the religious authorities. In one incident a paralytic man was lowered on a mat directly in front of Jesus. Upon seeing this Jesus said, 'Friend, your sins are forgiven'" (Luke 5:18).

The Pharisees quickly responded that only God could forgive sins, so in their eyes Jesus was committing blasphemy. Jesus knew what they were thinking and asked, "Why are you thinking these things in your hearts? Which is easier to say, 'Your sins are forgiven,' or to say, 'Get up and walk'? But that you may know that the Son of Man has authority on earth to forgive sins . . ." He said to the paralyzed man, "I tell you, get up, take your mat and go home." (Luke 5:18).

The core issue was simple. Was Jesus the Son of God, the Messiah? Is He God? Jesus said He was the Son of God. The Jewish leaders would reject His claim. When Jesus said, "Before Abraham, I am," they realized that He was claiming He was one with God. Their response was to immediately pick up stones to stone Him, declaring that He had blasphemed.

At another time Jesus said to them, "'My Father is always at his work to this very day, and I, too, am working." For this reason the Jews tried all the harder to kill him; not only was he breaking the Sabbath, but he was even calling God His own Father, making Himself equal to God" (John 5:16-18).

At His trial, just the mention from the lips of Jesus that He was Son of God was enough to condemn Him. They would accept no proof! Nothing He could do would convince them He is the Son of God. To them it was blasphemy, a charge serious enough to condemn Jesus to death.

These are just a few of the issues that made Jesus an outlaw to the land and people He came to share His truth with. It did not take long for them to make Him and outlaw – an outlaw they wanted to rid themselves of.

Jesus, the Outlaw, had to be silenced.

Applications from the Outlaw

Their voices were loud as they tried to drown out His voice, but they could not. The critics of Jesus were so busy telling Him who they thought He was, and whom He wasn't, that they forgot to listen! Are you listening to Him?

The truths He spoke about Himself have not changed. He said He is the Son of God. He said He can forgive our sins. He said He is coming back again. If that makes Him an outlaw in your life, so be it! Let Jesus do the talking and allow Him to tell us not only who He is, but also why He came.

Those who try to mold Jesus into the shape they want Him in and listen selectively to what they want to hear will usually try to get rid of Him in the end. Listen to His words and obey!

A Prayer

Jesus, may I not come to You with preconceived ideas, but with an openness to your revelation to me daily. Show me who you are and want you want me to do. In doing so – live within me!

Chapter Six

"When they could not manufacture a personal scandal discrediting Jesus . . . aside from calling Him a Samaritan, An ingenious but evil plan was conceived."

The Plot to Discredit Jesus, the Outlaw

There were four plots designed in all. The first was to discredit Him.

One of the best ways to ruin someone's reputation is to discredit him. There were several attempts to discredit Jesus. Each attempt was an effort to cast Him in a negative light so that the common people would not accept him. The authorities perceived Jesus as dangerous and a charlatan. They attempted to cast Him in the role of "outlaw."

First, they looked into Jesus' "dirty laundry" but came away with nothing. There was no scandal, no personal infidelity, or anything that they could use against Him which would hurt His reputation. The religious leaders were stymied. How could they discredit a Man whom others believed to be a prophet or Messiah?

Jesus was known for his miracles of healing the sick and lame, and raising the dead. The religious leaders decided to portray his miracles as a hoax. One example of this attempt is in John chapter nine. A blind man was presented to Jesus. Jesus spits on the ground, makes some mud with the saliva, and puts it on the man's eyes. "Go wash in the Pool of Siloam," Jesus tells the blind man. The man did as he was told and regained his sight (John 9:6-9).

The Jewish leaders wasted no time trying to discredit Jesus' healing power. In John 9:18, it was recorded that they sent for the man's parents, and questioned them at length, doubting the truthfulness of their story. They questioned the blind man, attempting to poke holes in his story. Then, giving up, they discredited Jesus by calling Him a sinner, to which the man answers, "Whether he is a sinner or not, I don't know. One thing I do know. I was blind but now I see!" Even the town people chime in that they remember that he was blind! As a last resort, the religious leaders claim that the man wasn't blind at all, and the whole thing is a hoax.

The scene ends as Jewish authorities threw the newly healed man out of the synagogue. If you wanted to believe in Jesus, you couldn't do it in the House of God! The man who was healed had become an outlaw. Jesus, knowing of the man's fate, did a wonderful and beautiful thing. Jesus sought the blind man out.

"And when he found him, he said, "Do you believe in the Son of Man?"

"Who is he sir?" the man asked. Tell me so that I may believe in him."

Jesus said, "You have now seen him, in fact, he is the one speaking with you."

Then the man said, "Lord, I believe," and he worshipped him. (John 9:35-38).

Ironic, isn't it? *A blind man saw Jesus for who He was, and the seeing men were blind to His identity.* The godly were thrown out of the synagogue, the place where one went to praise and to seek God.

It became difficult for the religious leaders to deny the miracles of Jesus. Too many people had witnessed them firsthand! The miracles were real and could not be denied; Lazarus being raised from the dead, the feeding of the five thousand, the healing of the paralytic, and the raising of the widow's only son from the dead were just a few that were witnessed. The Jewish leaders could no longer persuade the people that the miracles hadn't happened.

When they failed to discredit Jesus' healing powers, the religious authorities tried a new tactic. They began to say the healings *might* have happened, but that they were not miracles. They argued miracles only came from God. Therefore, they reasoned Jesus was in league with Beelzebub, the supreme evil spirit operating in the world, and was Satan incarnate. A more serious accusation could not have been laid at the feet of Jesus. Jesus claimed His kingdom was from above;

they would now claimed His kingdom was from below. *He claimed His kingdom was good, holy, pure and they declared His kingdom to be evil.* Jesus and His critics could not be more polarized.

As they moved to put this new scheme into place, Jesus drove out a demon from a man who could not talk. Then the man immediately began to speak. The crowd was amazed and said, "Nothing like this has ever been seen in Israel." (Matthew 9:32-33). The Pharisees immediately countered, "It is by the prince of demons that he drives out demons." (Matthew 9:34). In another passage, others tested him after his miracle by asking for a sign from heaven." (Luke 11:14-16).

Jesus' answered His critics by insisting in Luke 11:17, "Any kingdom divided against itself will be ruined, and a house divided against itself will fall. If Satan is divided against himself, how can his kingdom stand? I say this because you claim that I drive out demons by Beelzebub, by whom do your followers drive them out? So then, they will be your judges. But if I drive out demons by the finger of God, then the kingdom of God has come to you."

The plot to discredit Jesus, and the plot to align Him with the Satanic Kingdom of Beelzebub, failed.

So, the Jewish leaders conceived an ingenious, but evil plan. They would kill Lazarus, whom Jesus had resurrected, because He was a walking advertisement of the miraculous power of Jesus. Everywhere Lazarus went, crowds gathered around to touch him and see the one Jesus had resurrected from the dead. This infuriated the religious leaders who were seeking to squelch the popularity and influence that Jesus had on the common people! Lazarus always drew a crowd, a crowd that was always directed back to the dynamic power and claims of Jesus as the Messiah.

The second plot to dispose of Jesus was directed at Lazarus. In the Gospel of John, we read that a dinner was being thrown to honor Jesus. Mary and Martha gave it just a few days before the Passover feast as a thank you to Jesus for the raising of their brother from the dead. We read, "Meanwhile a large crowd of Jews found out that Jesus was there and came, not only because of Him, but also to see Lazarus, whom he had raised from the dead. So the chief priest made plans to kill Lazarus as well, for on account of him many of the Jews were going over to Jesus and putting their faith in him" (John 12:12). However, Lazarus remained safe. Another plot by the Jewish leaders was foiled!

With their plots to discredit Jesus in tatters, Lazarus safe, and Jesus refuting their claims that He was of the devil, the religious leaders decided to take a more drastic step.

They decided to kill Jesus.

Applications from the Outlaw

We discredit Jesus when we do not accept Him for whom and what He claims to be. We discredit His Holy name when we use it in unholy ways. That which diminishes the power of Jesus discredits His effectiveness in our lives. In this way, we make Him an outlaw to ourselves.

A Prayer

Father, Never let me never diminish the power of your Son in my life, But may I know within my heart That all things are possible Through Him, In things great and small Obvious or hidden.

CHAPTER SEVEN

"The plot to murder Jesus was the boldest
plan in history, We can blame others for His
death, But if we comprehend the message of the
Apostle Paul, *It is clear that the hammer and
nails are held in our hands!*"

THE PLOT TO MURDER JESUS,
THE OUTLAW

The plot to murder Jesus was the boldest
act ever planned and executed in history. In our
tolerant society, we seem too sophisticated to
murder someone who claims to be a messiah.
However, Americans have been known to
assassinate their prophets! If Jesus came back to

earth today in physical form, I am convinced that he would be murdered again.

The plot to murder Jesus was based on fear. It was a fear of the high priests, the Sanhedrin, and the Pharisees that Jesus would upset the precarious peace that Israel had negotiated with Rome. It was also trepidation on the part of the religious Jews that Jesus would destroy the traditions of Jewish religion and Law, and that the Temple would no longer be the center of the Jewish religion. Both the leaders of Jewish politics and leaders in Jewish religion would find that fear united them as allies in the common desire to get rid of Jesus.

At first the plot was to silence Jesus, to quiet His voice. However, when they realize that His influence was vast and that it seemed that the whole world had gone out to Jesus they became convinced that He must die.

Jesus knew that His death was imminent. However, Jesus was determined to give up His life according to His own timetable, and not theirs. He acted accordingly to avoid his untimely death by purposely staying away from Judea. Jesus refused to be a victim and stated several times in

the Gospel of John that His time had not yet
come. As the Feast of Tabernacles approached He
declared to His disciples, "The right time for me
has not yet come; for you any time is right . . .
You go to the Feast. I am not yet going up to this
Feast, because for me the right time has not yet
come" (John 7:6-8). Jesus did go to the feast in
His own time, and by his own route, avoiding an
untimely seizure and crucifixion. In John 7:30,
it says again that at the feast they "tried to seize
him but no one laid a hand on him, because his
time had not yet come. Still, many in the crowd
put their faith in him."

Later, the temple guards are sent back to
arrest Jesus, but the guards come back empty-
handed. The leaders are irate at the inability of
the guards to do their job, and chastise them,
saying, "You mean he has deceived you also?"

Unfortunately for the religious leaders, the
popularity of Jesus among the common people
was growing. Even though John said disciples
began to leave Him because of some of His
difficult teachings, His appeal was still huge. The
crowds formed because He was controversial and
notorious. Some people thronged around Him in

faith, others came because of their curiosity. To some degree, the mobs of people protected Jesus from being arrested.

As the popularity of Jesus grew, so did the anxiety of the religious leaders. How much power and influence would Jesus exert over the people? How would He use such power? Would such power be used against them? They believed the answer was a definite yes! According to John, these sentiments came to a head when some Jews went to the Pharisees and tell of Lazarus being raised from the dead. In John 11:47-49, we read: "Then the chief priest and the Pharisees called a meeting of the Sanhedrin. 'What we are accomplishing?' they asked. 'Here is this man performing many miraculous signs. If we let him go on like this, everyone will believe in him, and then the Romans will come and take away both our place (the Temple) and our nation.' "

From that moment on, the leaders no longer wished to just silence Jesus, they began to plot to take His life. And as a consequence, we read in John 11:53-54a: "Therefore Jesus no longer moved about publicly among the Jews. Instead he withdrew . . .. "

This is the first mention of a plot to kill Jesus. Notice that the religious leaders were concerned about the political ramifications of Jesus' popularity. They believed He would challenge the peace they had negotiated with the Romans — a peace they dare not jeopardize.

Soon the plot to take the life of Jesus was quite public. In John 7:25, the crowd muttered, "Isn't this the man they are trying to kill?" In John 8:40, Jesus showed he was aware of their plot, saying, "As it is, you are determined to kill me, a man who has told you the truth that I heard from God."

The plot to murder Jesus was in full swing. The religious leaders had set the trap, and wouldn't rest until Jesus was arrested and executed. They wondered if He would take the bait.

Applications from the Outlaw

We kill Christ every day through our own faults, failures and transgressions. This is the startling truth. We kill him and continue doing so. Our intimate and personal encounter with Him doesn't begin until we take responsibility for this fact.

A Prayer

Jesus, you have made the supreme sacrifice for me. Let me never take that lightly. As I live my life, forgive me that my words and actions often pain you and still crucify you!

Chapter Eight

"Jesus did not lie to His disciples
About what lie ahead of them.
Perhaps if they knew the Truth they
might not Have followed."

Jesus Warns His Disciples
about Becoming Outlaws

The Apocrypha tells about a man who died
and visited hell. When he got there, he was quite
surprised at what he found. Instead of a hot place
of eternal torment, hell was a very plush resort.
There was an abundance of lavish food, and wine

and liquor flowed like a river. People were gambling, and beautiful, sensual women were everywhere. Then, the man went to heaven, which was quite boring compared to what he saw in hell. When given a choice, he chose to go to hell as soon as possible.

However, when he arrived in hell, the casinos were gone, the women were ugly, the place was as hot as an oven, and every one appeared to be suffering. He was shocked, and asked the keeper of the gate if he could change his mind. The answer was quick and firm. "Absolutely not!"

"But I was just here a short time ago," he asked, completely puzzled. "What happened?"

"Oh, that," replied the keeper, "That was an advertisement!"

There are many scams in the world to get sucked into. What something appears to be may not be what we get. Some individuals learn this the hard way. We are often promised something, and then walk away feeling tricked. Life is sometimes a bait and switch!

Jesus never lied to His disciples. He told them from the beginning that following Him would be no picnic. Even though He was honest with them about the costs of discipleship, they did not fully realize the consequences of following Him. The resurrection of Christ and persecution of the early church was still in the future. Perhaps, if they had fully known what it meant to follow a Man who was an outlaw and criminal, they would have run away and not looked back! Later, when they were persecuted for their beliefs, they must have remembered Jesus words. He had warned them.

Heaven is a popular place that most of us want to go, but few people want to do what it takes to get there. In Matthew 7: 13-14, Jesus said, "Enter through the narrow gate. For wide is the gate and broad is the road that leads to destruction and many enter through it. But small is the gate and narrow is the road that leads to life and few find it." This was an apt illustration that the people understood, for every city had a gate or several gates which would allow travelers in or out of the city. But entering through the small gate is not easy, and traveling on the narrow road is difficult. The small gate and the narrow road aren't very popular!

The image of Jesus is often distorted to show him only as a peacemaker and a man of love. *We choose to ignore the Jesus who asks us to do things that are difficult.* What would you do if Jesus asked you to go to the cross with Him? Would you have the courage to follow?

Following Jesus cost his followers their homes. One day, when a would-be disciple came to Jesus, he promised, "Teacher I will follow you wherever you go." Jesus replied, "Foxes have holes and birds of the air have nests, but the Son of Man has no place to lay his head" (Matthew 8:19-20).

There was sadness in His response. The earth was no home for Jesus or those who followed him. From birth, they sought to kill Him. In Nazareth, His hometown, they forced Him to the edge of the city to throw Him off a cliff. He heard persistent rumors that the authorities sought to capture Him to put Him to death. His own family was divided over whether He really was the Messiah. When Jesus declared the Son of Man had no place to lay his head, it was more than a statement. It was an emotional expression of loneliness.

To follow Jesus was to become an outlaw. Jesus declared, "I am sending you out like sheep among the wolves. Therefore be as shrewd as snakes and as innocent as doves" (Matthew 10:16). He continued, "Be on your guard against men; they will hand you over to the local councils and flog you in their synagogues. On my account you will be brought before governors and kings as witnesses to them and to the Gentiles. But when they arrest you, do not worry about what to say or how to say it" (Matthew 10:20). Jesus described how family unity would be destroyed as brother betrayed brother, and children rebelled against their parents. Jesus made it clear that "A student is not above his teacher, nor a servant above his master. It is enough for the student to be like his teacher, and the servant like his master. If the head of the house has been called Beelzebub, how much more the members of his household" (Matthew 10:24-25). Then Jesus made one of His strongest statements: "All men will hate you because of me, but he who stands firm to the end will be saved" (Matthew 10:22).

Perhaps, it was fortunate that the disciples did not fully understand the impact of what Jesus was saying.

Imagine that you are in a Sunday school class at a local church seeking information on Christianity. Not much effort is usually required. Attend church, support the church financially, live a good life. Now, picture yourself in a class where the minister tells you that everyone who follows Christ will have a life of constant hardship. Your family will turn against you. You may lose your job. You might be hunted, persecuted, and possibly suffer a terrible death as a criminal. You may become an outlaw. How many do you think would join the church? How long do you think the church board would allow the minister to go before he is censored?

Would you still want to follow Jesus? Would you be willing to become an outlaw?

Jesus said his disciples would be handed over to be persecuted and put to death. He told them all nations would hate them. He was candid about what was in store for them.

But there was good news too! Jesus challenged His disciples to do everything He commanded of them and to remember, " if I go and prepare a place for you, I will come back and take you to be with me that you also may be where I am" (John 14:3). He also promised that they would have value: "So don't be afraid; you are worth more than many sparrows." (Matthew 10:31). Jesus told them they would always have the power of God with them. He reminded them that the Spirit would speak to them and tell them what they needed to say in difficult situations. They were outlaws and criminals, but they were never forsaken.

God continues to be with us today. I remember the time I had just finished a seminar on angels and Margaret, a delightful older woman, came up to me and asked if she could tell me her angel story. As a young girl, Margaret went to South America as a missionary for the Methodist Church. She had fantasized about what it meant to be a missionary, but once she was there, she became discouraged. The bugs were aggressive, it was extremely hot, the food nothing to write home about, and regular personal hygiene was difficult. One day she was sent alone to a village about four miles away. As she walked, she became sweaty and discouraged. She began to cry, and shouted, "God, what am I doing in this God forsaken place?"

Suddenly she knew she wasn't alone. She felt as if someone was there with her, watching her. This intense feeling increased until she felt that someone or something she could not see was standing directly in front of her. Then she felt something touch her on both arms and pull her forward. Her head stopped and rested on something. She realized a celestial being she could not see was hugging her. It held her tightly.

Then there was a soft but distinct voice that whispered in her ear. It was unmistakable, "We love you, we really love you. Even the Father loves you!"

The presence and the dynamic words were overpowering. She no longer doubted herself or wondered why she was there. She realized that she was not alone. She was loved by God's angels and by God as well. It was a life-changing message. Whenever I am feeling down, whenever I lose the vision, I replay this story of Margaret in my mind.

There were great rewards for being God's outlaws. Paul said, "I consider that our present sufferings are not worth comparing to the glory that will be revealed in us" (Romans 8:18). To Timothy, a young follower of Jesus, Paul said at the end of his tremendous journey of faith, "I have fought the good fight. I have finished the race, I have kept the faith. Now there is in store for me the crown of righteousness . . . " (II Timothy 4:7-8a).

Jesus warned His disciples of what was in store for them. *They discovered His words were true. They were hunted, betrayed, and martyred.*

They were outlaws.

Applications from the Outlaw

Jesus was honest about what is required to follow him. The road of discipleship is a difficult one, filled with obstacles. There will be valley experiences, and mountain top experiences. We may be persecuted, or members of our families may turn against us.

So why follow? It is because there is a love bond between Jesus and His followers. Love becomes the powerful motivation to serve Him and to endure all of the hardships. The challenge for us is to serve not out of obligation but desire, the desire to please God. When that happens we can not get enough of God and His kingdom. We choose to follow because we are promised an eternity with God and Jesus, His Son, as a reward for being faithful.

A Prayer

Father, I follow your Son freely knowing that it will be difficult at times, yet knowing I will never be left alone to fend for myself. The power of your love Sustains me!

Chapter Nine

"He knew they were waiting for Him.
He knew they wanted His life, but He went
anyway—knowing He must Defend the Honor
of His Father's House."

The Outlaw Invades
the Temple

If Jesus was a minor outlaw before He
entered the Temple, by the time He left, *He was
one of the biggest outlaws* to ever step foot inside.
Jesus' actions at the Temple drove the final nail
into His own coffin. He boldly stepped into the
mouth of the lion.

The enemies and critics of Jesus – the political Jews – used the Temple as a headquarters. It was the seat of the Sanhedrin, the political and judicial administration of Jewish law. It was also the seat of the financial administration, which handled the vast sums of the taxation and the offerings given to the Temple. The temple was the core, the focus point of their entire religious life. Here was found the current High Priest as well as all of the chief priests.

In the Gospel of John, we read that Jesus entered the Temple and caused chaos. He scattered the tables of the moneychangers, telling them, "Get them out of here! How dare you turn my Father's house into a market?" (John 2:16). Tables were overturned, doves flew out of their cages, animals escaped, and merchants scurried for cover. All of this happened at one of the busiest times in the temple, during the feast of the Passover. Jesus certainly had an audience to witness His anger and message. Jesus even made a whip and swirled it around His head, driving the merchants and moneychangers out of the Temple. "It is written, My house will be a house of prayer, but you have made it a den of robbers,'" (Luke 19:45). Immediately after He said these words, the chief priests, the teachers of the law, and the leaders of the people sought to kill him. But they could not carry out their plan, because the crowd hung on to Jesus' every word.

Does this story seem harsh to you? The Jesus of four Gospels who cleansed the temple of its moneychangers was an outlaw. Can we accept Jesus in this role? Or do we more comfortable with the concept of a peace- love Jesus? Yet, this incident is so important, all four Gospel writers recorded it.

Jesus was angry at the deception of the religious leaders. He was angry about the hypocrisy He saw in the Temple. He was angry with those who emphasized the letter of the Law. *He was angry at injustice. He was especially angry with those who took what was holy and dragged it into the gutter.*

What was it that made Him angry on this particular day? There were *two* possibilities. It appears that the buying and selling was happening not outside of the temple but inside the temple –

specifically in the Court of the Gentiles. Jesus appears to be angry that the temple a place of worship had become a place of business. The other possibility is that Jesus was angry about the prices for the offerings, which were exorbitant. Many innocent worshippers were forced to purchase the "accepted" offerings at their higher prices. The moneymakers and the temple officials had developed a profitable, corrupt system that enriched them. This is why Jesus called them a "den of robbers." He knew what was really happening at the temple under the guise of holiness was a farce. He called them on it in the most dramatic way possible.

Politically, what Jesus did at the temple seemed foolish. *Morally and spiritually it was the right thing to do.* It was an attack on their power and He hit them in their most vulnerable spot — their pocketbooks! However, Jesus was not intending to reform the temple by His confrontation. *He was passing judgment* on the temple and way it was run. He was condemning what it had become. Only Jesus had a right to do this.

When Jesus said, "Destroy this temple, I will raise it again in three days" (John 2:19) He was saying that He would replace the temple. In the past, the people had used the temple to approach and worship God; now Jesus would be their temple. When He died upon the cross, the temple curtain was torn apart that separated the people from the God, represented by the Holy of Holies. Now, God was approachable through the Temple of Jesus.

Had Jesus made a mistake by marching into the temple? The chief priests and Sanhedrin who were already plotting against Jesus were delighted. If they paid Him it could not have worked out any better! By his actions in the Temple, Jesus appeared to be out of control, which would help the religious authorities in their quest to silence him. Now they would have more than enough ammunition to solicit others to get rid of such a menace. The truth is that Jesus knew what He was doing, and He was in complete control of Himself. His disciples were shocked and knew it meant trouble. It appeared as if Jesus was walking into the jaws of death! But His disciples or public opinion did not control Jesus. It is through the voice of His Father that He had authority.

By His actions in the Temple, His status as an outlaw was elevated to a higher level. *He was now the Most Wanted Man in Israel.*

Applications of the Outlaw

We must keep what is holy in our lives holy. We must also do what is morally right at times even though we know there may be a high price attached to it. Seldom do we hear today that our bodies are the 'holy temples of God.' Yet, as we understand this truth, we will keep our mind and heart pure and uncontaminated by that which will harm it or make it impure. This especially means our bodies should be pure from addiction to sex, drugs, alcohol, or any substance, which seeks to master us.

Through Jesus, we can approach God and worship Him!

A Prayer

Loving God, help me to recognize my body as your holy temple. Help me to be careful what goes into my temple as well as what comes out. Help to keep the temple you have given to me – Pure.

Chapter Ten

"We could be critical of Judas
And damn him to hell for
Betraying Jesus, but perhaps there
Is a Judas in each of us
To be tamed?"

Judas Betrays the Outlaw

In an ancient document, there is a story about the young Jesus playing with some young boys. One of the boys hit Jesus on the side, and injures Him. Jesus cries out in pain. In the story, the young boy is Judas, and the side he hit Jesus on is the side where the Roman soldier thrust his spear into Jesus as He hung on the Cross.

The High Priests and religious leaders made it known that they wanted to arrest Jesus. Spies were sent to stand outside of the crowds that hovered to hear Jesus, looking for a weak link among His disciples. As they stood on the fringes of the crowd, they spread their poison and doubt into the minds of anyone who would listen.

In Luke 22:4, we read that *Judas makes the first move*. He approached the authorities, and discussed how much money they would pay him, and the details of the betrayal. "What are you willing to give me if I hand Him over to you?" (Matthew 26:15). The religious leaders were delighted, and quickly agreed to give Judas thirty pieces of silver up front. From that moment scripture says, Judas "was watching for an opportunity to hand Jesus over to them when no crowd was present" (Luke 22:6). He was obligated to follow through. The money was in Judas' pocket, and Judas was in their pocket. His betrayal was not an impulsive act of aggression. Rather, it was cold, calculating, and premeditated.

Judas led a crowd to the Garden where Jesus was praying. Within the crowd were soldiers of the Sanhedrin who came armed to take Jesus by force. So that there would be no mistake, Judas and the High Priests devised a sign. It was a kiss, universally accepted as a symbol of love. Judas would make it a sign of betrayal.

Judas had told them "The one I kiss is the man; arrest him." Going at once to Jesus, Judas said "Greetings, Rabbi!" and kissed him (Matthew 22:49). Jesus asks them, "Who is it you want?" (John 18:4). "Jesus of Nazareth," they replied. "I am He," Jesus said. (And Judas the traitor was standing there with them.) When Jesus said, "I am He," they drew back and fell to the ground. Again he asked them, "Who is it you want?' And they said, "Jesus of Nazareth." "I told you that I am He," Jesus answered. "If you are looking for me, then let these men go" (John 18:5-8).

It is clear that they were afraid of Jesus even up to the time of His arrest. Before the arrest they were afraid of the crowds, and didn't want to start a riot. But here, the guards and the *"swat team"* showed they were fearful of what Jesus might do — or even of His power.

Jesus was insulted that they had come out against Him as an outlaw. They came armed, expecting a fight, ready for a fight, and believing they could win such a conflict. Jesus was indignant. Listen to how he chastised them, "Am I leading a rebellion, that you have come with swords and clubs? Every day I was with you in the temple courts and you did not lay a hand on me. But this is your hour – when darkness reigns" (Luke 22: 52).

Jesus was treated like an outlaw, even though He didn't act like one. He took the initiative. Rather than hiding, Jesus assertively greeted them. The Garden is dark, yet Jesus stepped into the light to ask them why and who they are looking for. When they say His name, He quickly said, "Here I am." He repeated this more than once.

Jesus looked at Judas, the disciple who had followed Him for three years over mountains and valleys until this moment and said, "Friend, do what you came for." Then the soldiers stepped forward, seized Jesus and arrested Him. But, all was not over yet, it was not to be this simple. There is a short fight. The followers of Jesus ask permission to defend Jesus and themselves. "Lord, should we strike with our swords?" (Luke 22:49).

An outlaw would run. An outlaw would fight. *Jesus told his disciples not to fight.* Then he

admonished Peter and told him to put away his
sword. Peter had already struck the servant
Malchus, who lost his ear in the fight. Jesus now
continued His unusual and supernatural behavior.
He stopped to heal the ear of the Malchus,
restoring him completely. *He offered Himself
up, and refused to fight,* He healed the injury of
an enemy in the midst of the battle. He asked
for the release of His disciples. He allowed Judas
to kiss Him, knowing his intentions. See how
subtly he took control of the situations that faced
Him.

What amazing, utterly transcending pro-
active behavior at such a critical moment in all of
history!

*He would fight but only on His terms and in
His own way.*

The High Priests, elders, and soldiers believe
that they are in control. After all they outnumber
the disciples! Yet, listen to what Jesus says to them:
"Do you not think I cannot call on my Father,
and he will at once put at my disposal more than
twelve legions of angels?" (Matthew 27:53). A
legion consists of six thousand soldiers. Jesus said
that He can command at a moment's notice

72,000 angels and they would come to protect Him instantly.

They had captured Jesus, but only His body. They would soon discover that his physical capture would give them so little of His heart and spirit. Could they carry out the next step in their plan to silence Jesus, the Outlaw?

Applications of the Outlaw

As a psychologist, I know that betrayal is one of life's most difficult experiences. Judas betrayed Jesus, but even then Jesus addressed Judas as 'Friend' when he came into the garden. Forgiveness is always available from God regardless of what we have done in life. Often, however, I find that many individuals have not forgiven themselves. Keep your heart pure so you don't betray those you love, or the God you claim to love.

A Prayer

Jesus, I know you knew the pain of betrayal, as I live my life may I always guard against betraying in any way the ones I love. As I am true to myself help me to not betray myself!

CHAPTER ELEVEN

*"Simon Peter is laughable, loveable, brilliant,
stupid, insightful and clueless.*
He is definitely one of a kind."

THE OUTLAW AND THE
COURAGEOUS COWARD

To say that Peter was a courageous coward sounds like a contradiction – and it is!   Peter's courage got him into situations, which showed his humanness. Peter was a man of contrasts. As part of the inner circle of Jesus' ministry, his home in Galilee was the base station for much of Jesus' work. Yet Peter was outspoken, impulsive, naïve, and presumptuous.

We read in the gospel accounts that Jesus healed Peter's mother-in-law. Later, at Caesarea Philippi, it was Peter that made the powerful revelation concerning Jesus, "You are the Christ, the Son of the living God" (Matthew 16:16). When Jesus walked on water, Peter tried it as well! But He was soon overwhelmed by the waves and the storm. But Jesus chastised him for his lack of faith. When Jesus shared His plan to go to Jerusalem to give up His life, it is Peter who discouraged Him.

Peter talked big. Before the crucifixion, Jesus told his disciples that where He was going, they could not follow. Peter replied, "'Lord, why can't I follow you now? I will lay down my life for you.' Then Jesus answered, 'Will you really lay down your life for me? I tell you the truth, before the rooster crows, you will disown me three times!' " (John 13:37-38). When Judas and the Temple guard come for Jesus, it is Peter that rose to the occasion in order to defend Jesus.

Peter seemed to be quite courageous up to this point! Then things began to fall apart.

After the arrest of Jesus in the garden, Peter followed at a safe distance, until he reached the courtyard of the High Priest. The night was chilly, and he moved close to the fire to warm himself. To his horror, members of the group that arrested Jesus recognized Peter! They confronted him, saying to each other, "This man was with them." Peter denied that he knew Jesus three times. The third time, it was recorded that Peter so vehemently disowned knowing Jesus that "he began to call down curses on himself" (Matthew 28:74).

As Peter denied Jesus, Luke 22:61 tells us, "The Lord turned and looked straight at Peter." The eyes of Peter and Jesus met. Peter would never forget the look of Jesus, as he perceived him at such a pivotal moment! I wonder what Peter was thinking? I wonder what Jesus was thinking?

Three years of Peter's dreams, hopes and aspirations were tied up in Jesus. When others fled, Peter stayed. Even after being recognized once, he stayed. When he was recognized the second time, he stayed.

The third time, when his eyes met those of Jesus, Peter went out and wept bitterly.

We must realize that Peter followed Jesus
Because he loved Him
Because of his desire to be loyal to Him
Because he was courageous.

And it was Peter's courage that put him in the most vulnerable place. He was tempted and tested and even fell. His courageousness lead him into situations where he proved to be a coward.

But Peter's commitment and courage would eventually win out. Peter went back to the disciples.

That particular day in history in the courtyard, Peter disowned the outlaw Jesus. But Jesus saw the courageous Peter, the Peter that was loyal and committed. *After his resurrection, Jesus would no longer live alongside of Peter, He would live within Peter.* Empowered by the spirit of Jesus, Peter would later boldly speak to large crowds, and thousands of people would become Christians through his words.

Fortunately for Peter the outlaw named Jesus would not disown him!

Applications from the Outlaw

It is easy to identify with Peter. He had a good heart and he meant well, but he always ended up with his foot in his mouth! God's kingdom is a place where individuals make mistakes, own up to them, and keep moving forward. Peter took ownership of his mistakes and asked for forgiveness. When he did he was forgiven. Forgiveness must be part of every human relationship we live, freely giving what we have received.

Remember, a saint only has to get up one more time than he falls!

A Prayer

Father, Forgive my blunders and shortcomings, and there are many. I often speak when I should be quiet. I often what I ought not.. Forgive me and grant me the strength to get up again!

CHAPTER TWELVE

*"The religious leaders who held Jesus
captive had control over His body,
but they had little control over His spirit and
His attitude.   He remained in control and
Free to the end".*

TWO OUTLAWS NAMED JESUS

Jesus wasn't the only outlaw we read about in scripture. At the time of Jesus' arrest, there was another "true" outlaw named Jesus Barabbas (Matthew 27:16). The name "Jesus" was possibly a common one in New Testament times. Barabbas was a notorious criminal, and the Gospel of Luke tells us he had been thrown into prison for murder and insurrection.

Two men named Jesus. One a political prisoner, one a religious prisoner.

Like a game of musical chairs, Jesus was dragged from one authority to another:

Annas,

Caiaphas,

the Sanhedrin,

Pilate,

Herod,

and then Pilate again.

All of this occurs before He is crucified.

Throughout these appearances, He was treated illegally—beaten, mocked, and condemned.

Yet despite his treatment, *Jesus did not act like an outlaw or criminal.* Jesus did not seek immunity, attempt to cut a deal, or plead for His life. He admitted he was the Messiah to the Sanhedrin. He told Pilate He was the King of the

Jews. He did not blame His fate on someone else. During His trial and crucifixion, the true spirit of Jesus came through. It surprised His captors often putting them on the defensive. Jesus was ready for what lied ahead.

Pilate desperately wanted to let Jesus walk away a free man. In Matthew 27:19, we read that Pilate's wife sent him an urgent message: "Don't have anything to do with that innocent man, for I have suffered a great deal today in a dream because of him." Pilate told the chief priests "You brought me this man as one who was inciting the people to rebellion. I have examined him in your presence and have found no basis for your charges against him. Neither has Herod, for he sent Him back to us; as you can see, He has done nothing to deserve death. Therefore, I will punish Him and then release Him!" (Luke 23:17).

The High Priest and the Sanhedrin pressed Pilate, saying that Jesus' claim to kingship is a threat to Roman rule. They played their trump card, "If you let this man go, you are no friend of Caesar. Anyone who claims to be a king opposes Caesar" (John 19:12).

Pilate knew at that moment that the Sanhedrin and other religious leaders were blackmailing him.

Pilate was caught. He had found Jesus to be innocent. In Matthew 27:17, he let the people decide, "Whom do you want me to release for you, Jesus Barabbas or Jesus who is called the Messiah?' The people chose Barabbas, the true outlaw. Pilate yielded to the will of the people, washed his hands of any guilt, and let Jesus go to the cross.

The religious authorities branded Jesus as an outlaw. Now they had what they sought all along - the order for His death.

Applications from the Outlaw

Life is unfair. The innocent Jesus was crucified; the outlaw Jesus Barabbas goes free. Our world today is also unfair. The sooner we accept its unfairness the better off we are. God understands our inequitable situations – He's been there! Even when Jesus is treated unfairly, he remains in control of His words and actions. He sets an example for us to follow. Like Barabbas, we are the sinners – and because of Jesus, we are free!

A Prayer

When I see what it cost to redeem me I am overwhelmed with thankfulness. May I show my gratitude in every word and action. Help me to accept the unfairness of life and realize that you came to right the wrongs I am often forced to live with.

Chapter Thirteen

"There is something haunting about
a man who was born among the poor,
accumulated no treasure on earth, and
buried in a borrowed tomb."

The Outlaw in the
Borrowed Tomb

It was over. Jesus, the Outlaw, was dead.

Jesus had died more quickly on the cross than
normal because of the terrible beatings he had
endured before his crucifixion. To ensure he was
dead, a soldier plunged his sword into Jesus' side.

His body was now ready for burial. However, when a known criminal was executed, the remains were either left unburied or placed in an unholy or dishonored place.

Where would Jesus be buried?

There is an interesting footnote found in the New International Version Bible: "The release of the body of one condemned for high treason, and especially to one who was not an immediate relative, was quite unusual." Mark 15:45, NIV Study Bible p.1527. The body of Jesus was handed over to Joseph of Arimathea. Nicodemus assisted him in the burial of Jesus.

Who was Joseph? Scriptures tell us that he was rich, a member of the Sanhedrin and was known as a righteous man. He lived in a town about twenty miles away from Jerusalem. It also says he was one waiting for the kingdom of God. He may not have been present at the Sanhedrin when Jesus first appeared before it. But it is clear that Joseph did not consent to the decision or actions of the Sanhedrin against Jesus (Luke 23:51).

Joseph was a believer in Jesus. In another place it says he was a secret disciple. By his courageous act of asking for the body of Jesus, he made a bold public statement.

Many non-biblical sources now claim that Joseph may have been the brother of Mary, the mother of Jesus. *If Joseph was Jesus' great uncle—a blood relative*—the body would have been more readily released to him, and Mary, Jesus' mother, would've facilitated this.

Pilate quickly honored the request of Joseph. Roman guards helped take the body down. Nicodemus and another member of the Sanhedrin assisted him. Jesus was buried in the unused tomb hewn in stone that was set aside for Joseph of Arimathea.

Death had claimed Jesus the outlaw, but God would soon reclaim Him!

Applications from the Outlaw

Have you ever wondered where you will be buried when you died, and who would be at your funeral? What would they say about you? Jesus came into this world with nothing and left the same way. He was born among the animals and was buried in a borrowed tomb. What was important to Him was not what He accumulated, but the work He accomplished when He was here.

What will you leave behind?

A Prayer

Wonderful Father, Help me understand that while possessions are important in my life, the legacy I must give is my love and deeds of love. What I lay at the foot of Your throne is my heart and my life.

CHAPTER FOURTEEN

"The guards were bribed to keep the biggest
event in history a secret. But the secret
wouldn't stay dead, And once resurrected –
No amount of lies could keep it buried."

THE OUTLAW LIVES AGAIN!

Even after His death, Jesus the outlaw
inspired fear. The high priest approached the
Roman ruler Pilate and complained that he was
afraid that the disciples of Jesus would come and
steal the body.

"Sir," they said, "we remember that while
he was still alive that deceiver said, 'After three

days I will rise again.' So give the order for the tomb to be made secure until the third day." Matthew 27:63-64.

The chief priests and the Pharisees feared Jesus even in his death. Pilate is tired of their problems. He had already mocked the Jewish leaders by inscribing above the head of Jesus', "Jesus of Nazareth, the King of the Jews" in Aramaic, Latin, and Greek, so it could be read by all who were there. The religious leaders were upset with this and wanted it to read "He SAYS He is King of the Jews." Pilate would not change the sign. Now, Pilate makes it clear he is finished with anything to do with Jesus. If they wanted to guard the Tomb, they would have to do it themselves. His exact words are "Go, make the tomb as secure as you know how" (Matthew 28:65). The Jewish leaders brought security guards from the Temple to guard the tomb, and then they sealed it by pushing the biggest stone they could find in front of it. The tomb of the outlaw was secure; void of light, void of air. Now they thought it was safe.

They weren't counting on supernatural powers!

The Temple soldiers guarding the tomb are possibly the *same* guards that encountered Him in the garden. And now, something is about to happen at the tomb of Jesus that would change their lives. It made the Temple guards infamous.

There was a violent earthquake caused by an angel of the Lord that came down from heaven. He went directly to the tomb, rolled back the stone and sat on it. His appearance was like lightning, and his clothes were dazzling white. The guards were so afraid of this angel that they were unable to move, paralyzed by fear. They became like dead men. Imagine! They were the very first to witness the resurrection of the outlaw Jesus. How that must have impacted them! *Those alive become like dead men, the dead Man becomes alive. How ironic!*

The temple guards were the first witnesses to the resurrection of Jesus!

The guards were helpless. They could not arrest Him as they did in the garden; they could not mock Him or beat Him as they did at the trial. *Human power over Jesus was finished forever.*

A few of the guards ran to the city to report the bad news to the high priests. Did this cause the high priests to believe? No! Don't ever underestimate human pride. Spiritual rigor mortis has set in, with tragic results.

They had to move quickly to cover up the resurrection of Jesus. "When the chief priests had met with the elders and devised a plan, they gave the soldiers a large sum of money, declaring to them, "You are to say, 'His disciples came during the night and stole him away while we were asleep.' If this report gets to the governor, we will satisfy him and keep you out of trouble" (Matthew 28:12-14). The soldiers took the money and did as they were instructed—they spread the lie.

The truth, the lie, the cover up, the pay off. It is amazing what money buys! Thirty pieces of silver bought information that led to the capture of Jesus, and now a large sum of money spread a lie about His resurrection. But it was impossible to keep the news of Jesus' resurrection a secret!

Applications from the Outlaw

This is the Jesus who declared "Because I live you shall live also." The resurrection of Jesus is the validation of everything He declared about

Himself and His kingdom. However, like the guards do you keep Jesus' resurrection a secret? Jesus died for each one of us. He gives to us the gift of eternal life. If we don't talk about it and share the good news, we, like the guards, will be guilty of a history's biggest cover up.

A Prayer

Jesus you are my loving Savior who has generously given all your treasures to me. May my words and my actions proclaim the good news of my new life in You.

Chapter Fifteen

"Bold . . . outspoken, boastful, Paul
treated the early Christians as outlaws.
But when he met Jesus, the ultimate outlaw,
He himself Became one of the most notorious
Outlaws of all!"

From Outlaw Hunter to Outlaw

Paul was the early Christian's worst nightmare. He was a leading Pharisee, dedicated to making the lives of Christians totally miserable. And he had the power and influence to do it!

We do not know a great deal about Paul. We do know he was originally called Saul, born into the tribe of Benjamin, and a zealous member of the Pharisees. He was a Roman citizen from Tarsus, a known region for academic study and Greek culture. Paul was educated in the Jewish faith at the feet of the respected rabbi Gamaliel. In physical stature he was not impressive, but what he lacked in looks he made up with his enthusiasm and spirit.

"Saul" first made an appearance in the book of Acts, chapter eight. Stephen, a follower of Christ, was being stoned, and his clothes were laid at the feet of Saul. Saul might have even been in charge of his execution! Acts 8:1 tells us, "And Saul was there, giving approval to his death." Saul was participating in murder.

Even as he breathed his last, Stephen fell on his knees and cried out, "Lord, do not hold this sin against them" (Acts 7:57). Augustine writes, "The Church owes Paul to the prayer of Stephen." Whether this is true or not, I believe Saul never forgot the words Stephen said as he died.

The death of Stephen marked the end of an era and the beginning of a new one. Great persecution broke out in Jerusalem, directed at the apostles. In Acts 9:1, we read, "Saul was still breathing out

murderous threats against the Lord's disciples."
This new, intense assault sent the apostles out
from Jerusalem and into the world. The death
of Stephen seemed to empower the Sanhedrin and
the chief priests. They, along with Saul, targeted
the Christians and the young Church in
Jerusalem. Acts 8:3 records that Saul went "from
house to house, he [dragging] off men and women
and [putting] them in prison." He acted as
prosecutor, judge, and jury. No trial necessary!

The Jewish church in Jerusalem
commissioned Saul to go to Damascus. In
Damascus, Saul planned to imprison Christians
as he had done in Jerusalem. As he neared
Damascus, the Scriptures say, "suddenly a light
from heaven flashed around him. He fell to the
ground and heard a voice say to him, "Saul, Saul,
why do you persecute me?"

"Who are you, Lord?" Saul asked.

"I am Jesus, whom you are persecuting," he
replied. "Now get up and go into the city, and
you will be told what you must do" (Acts 9:3-6).

Saul had treated God's people as criminals
and outlaws. Now, he had just encountered the
greatest outlaw of them all: Jesus Christ! This

vision was just for Saul because the others traveling with him heard the sound but did not see anyone.

Saul got up from the ground and found that even though he opened his eyes, he could not see. Saul was blind! Now they must lead him by the hand into the Damascus. He thought he was going to ride into Damascus with power and authority. Now he came in humility and in total blindness. He was both spiritually and physically blind. *Only now, Saul has the possibility of seeing the truth.*

How quickly God, through His Holy Spirit and His Son, can turn us around! *In a moment's notice God gives us a new reality!* We can be on a path *we* believe is right, and God can spin us around one hundred and eighty degrees and send us in a different direction.

As a psychologist, I often see firsthand how difficult it is to have what one believes to be true, shattered suddenly. Imagine a bridge being supported by two large pillars of cement which are suddenly torn away!

This was the case with Jeremy. When he came to me, he was still estranged from his father, who had abandoned him at a young age. His mother painted his birth father as a terrible man who had abused her. One day, Jeremy picked up the phone and overheard his mother talking to Jack, his birth father. His mother was telling Jack that Jeremy did not want to talk to him and he already had a new father. She asked him to not call again. Jeremy discovered that everything his mother and step-father had said about his father were lies. The people he loved and trusted had betrayed him! His father had not abandoned him, she had abandoned his father. There was no domestic abuse. Jeremy eventually went to live with his father, but oh! the pain of the crumbling structure he had built his life upon. How could he possibly make up for those lost years?

Most of what Saul had believed was suddenly proved false. What he believed as false was shown to him to be true. God has a way of doing this. He can change our reality in an instant, and it will drastically change us. But when change like this occurs, it throws the person into crisis.

Saul was suddenly in crisis, but he was quickly given a new foundation and structure for his life. Saul accepted the claims of Jesus Christ, the person he had hunted. He accepted that Jesus had risen; Jesus was the Messiah; Jesus was the Son of God; and that Jesus took priority over the Temple and the Law. He even changed his name to Paul to reflect his new commitment to Christ.

And Saul—now Paul—had become an outlaw.

Jesus later appeared to Paul while he was in Jerusalem, praying in the temple. In a trance, Paul saw Jesus speaking to him telling him to "Leave Jerusalem immediately, because they will not accept your testimony about me" (Acts 22:18). In the same trance Jesus says, "Go; I will sent you far away to the Gentiles" (Acts 22:21). Paul would later tell the churches he spoke to that his authority came from the fact that he had seen and encountered Jesus.

Paul had a new mission in life: to be the apostle to Gentiles to bring the good news of Jesus Christ. In this effort, Paul made three major missionary journeys. These journeys span 46 AD to 57 AD, with Paul traveling through what is modern Turkey, Macedonia, Cyprus, Athens, Sicily, and portions of Italy. During his last journey, Paul wrote the biblical book of *Romans*, a powerful foundation of the Christian faith. He also wrote many letters to the church at Corinth.

Paul described the life of the Christian this way, "We are hard pressed on every side, but not crushed; perplexed, but not in despair; struck down, but not destroyed. We always carry around in our body the death of Jesus, so that the life of Jesus may also be revealed in our body. For we who are alive are always been given over to death for Jesus' sake, so that his life may be revealed in our mortal body. So then, death is at work in us, but life is at work in you" (2 Corinthians 4:8-12).

He encountered hardships. In his letter to the Corinthians, Paul talked of Christians who boasted in their sufferings. Paul felt he had endured more in comparison and wrote to set the record straight. "I have worked much harder, been in prison more frequently, been flogged more severely, and been exposed to death, again and again. Five times I received from the Jews the forty lashes minus one. Three times I was beaten with rods, once I was stoned, three times I was shipwrecked, I spent a night and a day in the open sea, I have been constantly on the move. I have been in danger from rivers, in danger from bandits, in danger from my own countrymen, in danger from the Gentiles, in danger in the city, in danger in the country, in danger from sea; and in danger from false brothers. I have labored and toiled and have often gone without sleep; I have known hunger and thirst and have often gone without food; I have been cold and naked. Besides everything else, I face daily the pressure of my concern for all the churches" (2 Corinthians 11:23-28).

We also know that Paul suffered from a "thorn in [his] flesh, a messenger of Satan, to torment [him]." While we do not know for sure what the origin of the physical problem was, it may have been an eye problem.

In Acts, we read that Paul made a final trip to Jerusalem. The leaders he once represented in persecuting the Christians had become Paul's greatest enemy. They had been waiting for Paul. To them, he had become an outlaw.

Paul was first charged with taking a Gentile into the restricted area of the Temple, thus defiling the Temple. Later, he was accused of being a troublesome person to them.

However, the real reasons Paul was arrested included his mission to the Gentiles, and his belief in resurrection—especially the resurrection of Jesus. Paul eventually became a prisoner of the Roman emperor. It is believed that he was executed about the same time as Peter.

In the end the hunter would become the hunted, the persecutor would become the persecuted. He who treated God's people as criminals became a criminal himself.

Outspoken, bold, aggressive – Paul was perhaps the biggest outlaw of all.

Applications from the Outlaw

God challenged everything Paul held as being true, and showed him that his beliefs were false. Sometimes, we need to challenge the things we believe are true. *Human pride and ego are what usually stand in the way of seeing a new reality.* Remember when you ask, God can change your life *immediately.* Accept Jesus in your heart, and ask Him how you can serve Him, and begin finding the truth.

A Prayer

Challenge me, O Lord, In those areas of my life where my ego and pride still stand in the way of our love. Help me to give up seeing the World and my life – My way, and see it through Your eyes.

Chapter Sixteen

"He invited them to take up their Cross and follow Him. At the time I wonder if they realized How literal His words *Really were!*"

The Disciples Become Outlaws

Danger was everywhere after the crucifixion of Jesus, and no one knew that better than His disciples. They met behind locked doors. Would they be executed next? The disciples fully realized at that moment how dangerous it was to follow Jesus.

Would they still choose to follow Him? Did they become outlaws? Here's "the rest of the story."

James, the brother of John

James, the brother of John, was the first apostle to suffer the fate of an outlaw. According to Clement of Alexandria, the early Christian historian, the soldier that brought James to the tribunal seat, where he was condemned to death, confessed to be a Christian. "And so they were lead for together, where in the way he desired of James to forgive him what he had done. After James had a little paused with himself upon the matter, turning to him he said, 'Peace be to thee, brother,' and kissed him. And both were beheaded together in A.D. 36."

Peter

Tradition tells us that Peter lost his life at the hands of the Roman Emperor, Nero. Nero's persecution began about 64 AD So intense and violent were his actions against the Christians that he was thought to be the antichrist! During this time of persecution, the great Apostle Peter meet his death. Legend says that there Peter sought to escape from Rome, and in disguise, he made his way to the city's gate. There, to his surprise, he met Jesus heading into the city.

"Lord where are you going?" Peter asked.

Jesus replied to him, "I am going to Rome to be crucified again."

With those words Peter was cut to the heart. He realized that Jesus wanted him to go back and die just as He had died.

Peter saw his wife led to her death, and it is said that called out her name and encouraged her, saying, "Think, my beloved, of the Lord." Peter's last prayer was these moving words: "We praise you, we give you thanks, and confess you, glorifying you, even we men who are without strength, for you are God alone and none other, to whom be the glory now and unto all ages, Amen!"

This faithful couple who lived alongside of Jesus and witnessed His death, joined Him in His kingdom.

Thomas

Thomas is said to have died in India, but not before he had preached to the Parthians,

Medes, Persians, Carmanians, Hyrcanians, and the Bactrians. Thomas was taken captive in the city of Calamina, India. Then, he was taken outside of the city to a high mountain by four soldiers, who pierced him with spears and put an end to his life. The once-doubting Thomas died, fully believing in the Jesus he followed.

Andrew

Andrew, the brother of Peter, died an unusual death. Aegeas, one of the governors of Rome asked the Senate to have all Christians sacrifice and honor Roman idols. Andrew, a verbal critic of this law, was brought before him. He told Aegeas that Jesus came into the world to save men and that the Roman gods were really enemies to mankind. By serving false gods, Andrew claimed that men fall into wickedness. After their death, they only leave evil deeds behind them.

The Governor Aegeas was furious. He ordered Andrew to stop preaching. Andrew responded with these words, "I would not have preached the honor and glory of the cross if I feared the death of the cross."

It is said that Andrew was lead to a hill where a cross awaited him. He turned to his executioners and stated, "Come you ministers of joy to me, you servants of Aegeas; accomplish the desire of us both, and bind the lamb to the wood of suffering, the man to the maker, the soul to the Savior."

Legend claims the cross he was crucified on was in the shape of an "X," which has become known as St. Andrew's cross.

Bartholomew

Bartholomew's accomplishments include his translation of the original Gospel of Matthew into the native tongue of the people he ministered to in India. It is believed that he accompanied Philip on many of his journeys. Legend has it that he was crucified and beheaded in Armenia.

Philip

Philip is reported to have spent his later years preaching in Hierapolis, Phyrgia. It is there he was stoned and then hanged on a hook, head downward, on a tree near the temple. He died at the age of eighty-seven and was buried with his daughter.

Matthew

Matthew is best known for writing the first Gospel to the Jews in the Hebrew tongue. His work was concentrated mainly in Ethiopia and all of Egypt. King Hyrtacus ordered him stabbed to death, but it seems that the order was not carried out. It is possibly that Matthew died a natural death and never faced martyrdom. However, he was hunted and treated like an outlaw until his death.

Simon and Judas, the son of James

Simon the Cananaean and Judas the son of James do not stand out in the Gospel accounts. Yet they paired up to do the work that Jesus commanded them to do, "Go out into all the world." It is said that they met their martyrdom in Persia. There they worked for thirteen years in the twelve provinces of the country. One of their converts, Craton, is said to have reported their work in ten books, which describes their travels brought them to the city of Suanir. There a great temple of the sun god was erected, ministered to by seventy priests. Knowing that "two Hebrews" were coming and they would destroy the temple with their preaching, two magicians, Zaroes and Arphaxat suggested to the priests that they compel the disciples to sacrifice to the sun god.

Brought before the priests, they refused. While they were discussing this among themselves, an angel of the Lord appeared to them saying, "Choose one of two things, either the death of the people gathered here, or the palm of your martyrdom." The apostles quickly replied, "Let the mercy of our Lord Jesus Christ be implored that it both grant them forgiveness and aid us to receive the crown by constancy."

When silence fell upon the crowd they informed them, "Hear all of you and see. We know the sun to be a servant of God, and the moon likewise to be subject to the command of the Creator. We cannot and will not worship them."

Furious, the priests and the people killed them. They died thanking God that they could suffer for His name.

James

James the son of Alphaeus is mentioned in Mark 15:40. The original Greek the word associated with James means "less or little." It is possible that James was short in stature. He was the son of Mary Cleophas whom scholars believe is mentioned in Mark 15:40 as watching the crucifixion from a distance. How he met his death is unknown, but we know his brother was crucified in Egypt by the Roman Emporer Trajan.

Judas

Judas Iscariot was the betrayer of Jesus, yet he was one of twelve disciples chosen to share His life and ministry. Judas was his own worst enemy. When Judas realized that the authorities intended to kill Jesus, Scripture says that "he was seized with remorse and returned the thirty silver coins to the chief priests and elders."

Then he went away and hung himself (Matthew 27:3-7).

But Judas' remorse and guilt does not drive him back to Jesus. Judas teaches us that even though we are sorry for what we do—and even if we do receive forgiveness—it can not undo the consequences of our actions.

Judas became an outlaw to himself.

Matthias

Matthias is the disciple that took the place of Judas. In the book of Acts, one of the first acts of the remaining eleven disciples was to elect another apostle to replace Judas Iscariot. Two men were nominated as candidates for that significant position. The disciples prayed "Lord, you know everyone's heart. Show us which of these two you have chosen to take over this apostolic ministry, which Judas left to go where he belongs." Then they cast lots. . ." (Acts 1:24-26).

The Old Testament method of casting lots would be to put stone or broken earthenware with the names on it into a jar. Then the jar would be shaken until one of the stones fell out. The piece of earthenware that fell out had the name of Matthias, who takes the place of Judas.

Legend has it that Matthias and Andrew teamed up for several journeys. According to one account, Matthias goes to the city of the Myrna to visit a church established by both he and Andrew. Even though he heals the son of Ziphagia and converts her, King Bulphamus has him arrested. He orders Matthias to be burned to death in the courtyard and his body thrown into in the Black Sea.

Matthias died a martyr's death.

John

John, the prolific writer of the Gospel and also the writer of the Book of Revelation, was one of the few disciples that did not die a violent death. Domitian became emperor in A.D. 81, and his reign brought persecution to the Church. John was a great leader at the church in Ephesus and clashed with the proconsul in Rome. John was commanded to deny Christ in accordance with the edict of Domitian. In reply he said, "It behooves us to obey God more than man, hence I will neither deny Christ nor desist from preaching his name, but continue the course of my ministry which I received from the Lord." As a result of this the Proconsul had John tortured, then exiled him to the small barren island of Patmos.

After a twenty day fast, John had a vision and wrote the Revelation of John. After Emperor Domitian died John was released and came back to Ephesus where he lived peacefully the rest of his life.

John claimed to have a vision of his death. Acting upon that vision he took two young men outside of the city gates of Ephesus. There, he had them dig his grave. After they were finished, he took off his garments. Then he prayed to Jesus, telling Him his task was over, and he looked forward to the salvation which was waiting for him. He turned to the sun rising in the east and declared, "You are with me, O Lord Jesus Christ." John then laid down in the trench dug for him, gave up his spirit and passed on. He was ninety-seven years old.

James, the brother of Jesus

This list would not be complete without including James, the brother of Jesus. Even though he is not listed as one of the first disciples, he played a significant role in the early church. He originally did not believe that Jesus was the Messiah, and only changed his mind when Jesus personally appeared to him as recorded in 1 Corinthians 15:7. He later became a pillar of the church, even ranking ahead of Peter. He governed the church of the apostles from Jerusalem.

There are many legends surrounding James. We do know that he became a leader in the Christian Church in Jerusalem. Hegesippus, an anti-Gnostic of c. 175 tells of James' martyrdom. James was described as a Nazarite who prayed day and night in the temple for the Jewish people.

According to Hegesippus, James was coerced to address a crowd of worshippers who had come during the Passover. They had him stand and speak from the pinnacle of the temple. The scribes and Pharisees wanted him to use his influence to stop people from leaving the Jewish faith to follow Jesus. But James foiled the plans of the leaders by declaring, "Why do you ask me of Jesus the Son of Man? He sits on the right hand of the Most High, and shall come in the clouds of heaven." Hearing this, many in the crowd praised Jesus. The angry scribes and Pharisees threw him down from the pinnacle. James lived, and asked God to forgive them, for they didn't know what they were doing. Finally, someone in the crowd came up and struck James on the head killing him. James ended his life believing and committing his life to Jesus his earthly brother, as Christ, the Son of God and Messiah.

Jesus' disciples discovered that what He shared with them was true – following Him would be difficult, even dangerous. They would be hunted, persecuted, and even brought before political leaders. Most would die as martyrs giving their life for the cause of Jesus. Yet, each one was totally committed to Jesus Christ. Their efforts turned the world upside down and changed the world forever.

They became outlaws—and they did it willingly!

Applications from the Outlaw

The disciples surprised themselves with their courage and boldness! What turned these cowards into heroes? The answer is simple—God's Holy Spirit.

The Holy Spirit allowed Jesus' disciples to be effective in their lives. Ask, the Holy Spirit is yours, as well!

A Prayer

Jesus, it is clear to me that following you will not be easy. Help me to pay the price with a willing and loving heart, and know the prize before me will be great!

CHAPTER SEVENTEEN

"The world that is ahead of us will see Jesus as
history's greatest enemy. The great shoot-out
will occur At the Battle of Armagaeddon
Where the followers of Jesus, The Outlaw
Will slay the Great Deceiver!"

JESUS, STILL AN OUTLAW

Jesus was an outlaw when he lived. He's still
an outlaw today, if we reject the truth about Him!

I recently did a book signing in my
hometown of Grand Rapids, Michigan. The local
newspaper did a review of my book, which was

buried in the Religion Section. On the front page of the newspaper, was an article about a theologian who claims the *Bible is not to be taken literally*. This theologian claimed that the Gospel writers, who proclaimed that Jesus is the Messiah, didn't have all their facts straight. He insisted that they wrote decades after his death and were advancing their own agendas. He also claimed that the miracles should be viewed figuratively, with spiritual messages, not as literal miracles.

So *figuratively*, he said, the empty tomb tells us that the spirit of Jesus is still present in our world. The feeding of the multitudes tells us that God's spirit can satisfy the hunger in our souls. Jesus' healing of the blind, and the sick shows us how the spirit of God enlightens and heals. He insisted there that Jesus didn't really walk on water, there was no real physical resurrection, and it was not a real Jesus who ascended into heaven.

The danger of looking at the New Testament account figuratively is that we take the miraculous power of God out of the Scriptures. *If we took the miracles out of the New Testament, we would be left with only conjunctions such as "and, but, and or."* We would have Jesus without the awesome, dynamic power of God behind Him. We would have a powerless Jesus.

Others like to insist that *Jesus is only one of several possible ways to God*. Recently, I listened to a man who illustrated his talk with a piece of blank paper, which he folded in half. He likened each side of the paper to our spiritual journey. He explained that some individuals and groups were climbing up from the one side while others were climbing from the other side. In the end we would all met on top. Many who walked out of that particular place of worship that day thought that the talk was very warm and reconciliatory.

This is the prevalent thinking in society. *Christianity* is seen as simply a religion among religions without any uniqueness.

According to this kind of thinking, the journeys of the apostles and especially the Apostle Paul were in vain. Instead of challenging the various religions along the way, they would like to have Paul saying "I believe in Jesus, but I see that you believe in the god of the sun. That is all right, you continue to believe in the god of the sun and I will believe in Jesus and in the end it won't matter. What matters is a pure heart and sincerity rather than the truth."

Humankind has had this problem from the beginning of time. It is an attempt to reverse what God accomplished in the Garden by making God in the image of humans. Thus God has been cast into the form of graven images, images on the level of man that we can more easily understand and relate to. The Greeks gave us gods with human characteristics, faults, and failures and the world was often their playground full of intrigue.

For example, when Moses was on the moutain receiving the Ten Commandments, the Hebrews were in the valley impatient with the absence of Moses. Soon with the help of Aaron, his brother they had constructed a golden calf. They wanted a god they could touch and see. Thus Israel's greatest moment was also their lowest.

Perhaps it is this mentality that seeks to mold and shape Jesus into the image that we want, rather than whom He really is.

Universalists believe there are many paths to God, and we should respect them all. This belief system is in direct contradiction to both the Old and New Testament. The Christian faith teaches there are eternal truths! Jesus came and revealed those truths to us. *Universalism* is making tremendous inroads into Christianity. As the world shrinks and we find ourselves alongside of other religions, it seems to be ecumenical thing to do. We need to recognize Universalism for what it is. It is a threat to the truths of Jesus Christ . *It will doom the movement of Jesus Christ!* It will have us believe that all doors lead to Jesus, all roads lead to His kingdom. It sounds good— but that's not what He said!

Who is Jesus, the outlaw, really?

Many individuals go to the Gospel accounts and want to *selectively choose* what they like and will accept as truth concerning Jesus. This accounts for most of the serene looking pictures in places of worship. One may choose a Jesus who is loving, kind, compassionate and non-abrasive, and totally disregard the Jesus who talks about the consequences of our sins.

Then there are the unpopular or difficult sayings such as loving our enemies and even praying for them. There is the encouragement to love the unlovely, to turn the other cheek if struck, even if they were wrong, to go the extra mile. When it comes to forgiveness you should forgive your brother or sister not once, but seventy times seventy. These are nice stories to read in church. But who wants to take ownership of them? These are unpopular sayings so we throw them away.

Jesus is an outlaw. This is the Man who ate with sinners, sat with tax collectors, and visited the homeless. He talked to prostitutes and to heathen people. He shared His words of wisdom with the poor. None of this was popular or proper according to the respectable religious leaders.

Jesus, the outlaw, makes these claims today:

- He claims to be the Son of God.

- He claims to be the Messiah.

- He claims He can still heal and perform miracles in our lives today.

- He claims we should totally accept Him and His kingdom on faith.

- He claims His kingdom is here now.

- He claims He rose from the dead and is coming back in glory to gather all those who believe in Him.

- He claims we will spend eternity with Him in His kingdom.

Our challenge is to accept Jesus on His terms, rather than changing Him and altering Him to fit into our lives. If we change His truths and water them down, He will be outlawed in our lives. We will push Him away.

Jesus the outlaw is alive and well. History has not quenched His power or diminished His appeal. It is time to allow Him to tell us who He is. Some still want Him dead, others would be content to simply rid Him from their lives because He demands too much. Yet, no human force in heaven or earth can now hold back the power of Jesus. Have no doubt that if He came back today, He would still be an outlaw, for what He claimed about Himself. *By rejecting His claims we become the smug religious leaders who persecute Him as an outlaw.*

If we accept His truths, understanding why He was and still is an outlaw, His truths may haunt us, but they will also inspire us and lead us to His eternal kingdom. Perhaps, our greatest return will be that we will not be outlawed to God!

Applications from the Outlaw

We are living in dangerous times. A time when our schools are not safe, when domestic abuse and violence are on the rise. Our homes are in jeopardy. There is violence in the workplace. Sexual scandals and corruption happen at every level of our society.

If we ever needed Jesus, the Outlaw, it is today. Only Jesus, the Outlaw, is the answer! Have you accepted Jesus on His terms?

A Prayer

Jesus, may I do nothing in my life to reject you. May the truths You shared about Yourself, be readily accepted in my life. May my words always be filled with Your praises as God's Divine Son.

Chapter Eighteen

The Death of the Outlaw, Revisited

I had a dream again . . . and this time . . .

I was standing on the sidelines of the crowd. The man called the Christ lifted His head. I could see a plaited crown of thorns pressed deep into his skull. Blood trickled down his forehead. His face was bathed in sweat. His eyes were dark, soft, penetrating and intense.

His eyes met mine. A warm sensation swept over me. His lips parted and I knew He was going to tell me something. I waited for the slash of the whip across His back to interrupt us as before, but it never came.

His voice was not much more than a whisper, and I heard it for the first time.

"I was willing to be an outlaw for you. Will you be an outlaw for me?"

His eyes were pleading.

I held my hand out to Him. A tear rolled down my cheek.

"Yes, Jesus. Yes! I will." I cried. My body trembled.

A whip from one of the soldiers lashed across His back, "Let's keep it moving," The soldier commanded. Down the narrow street they progressed towards the hill called Golgatha. . ."

I awoke. The dream had seemed so real! I lay there, motionless. My sheets were soaked in sweat. It is then I opened my hand and discovered *I held a thorn stained with blood.*

BIBLIOGRAPHY

Barclay, William. *Discovering Jesus*. Louisville, KY: Westminster John Knox Press, 2000.

The Bible Through the Ages. Pleasantville, New York: The Reader's Digest Association, 1996.

Daniel-Rops, Henri. *Daily Life in the Time of Jesus*. New York: Hawthorn Books, 1962.

Foxe, John. *The New Foxe's Book of Martyrs*. Ed. Harold Chadwick. North Brunswick, NJ: Bridge-Logos Publishers, 1997.

Keyes, Nelson Beecher *Story of the Bible World*. Pleasantville, New York: The Reader's Digest Association, 1962.

Kraeling, Emil G. *The Disciples*. Rand McNally, 1966.

ABOUT THE AUTHOR

Thomas A. Bruno is a graduate of Hope College, Western Theological Seminary and The Center for Humanistic Studies. He has a Master's Degree in Divinity and holds a specialist degree in Clinical Psychology and Humanistic Education. Bruno began his private practice in 1991.

Bruno has served several Reformed, Presbyterian, and Congregational Churches. He is presently a minister with standing in the Congregational Church.

He appeared on *Oprah Winfrey* as a guest expert on men's issues and the *Shirley Show* in Canada. He and his wife Michele live in Troy, Michigan. He is presently working on several writing projects, including a book on abuse and a novel.

JESUS
Ph.D.
PSYCHOLOGIST

*Never Was a Man More in Control of
His Emotions, His Feelings, His Thoughts
& His Actions*

*Over Thirty Easy-to-Read Insights
With Life-Changing Answers*

TOM BRUNO